Brain Based Learning and Special Education

Dr. Clyde Winters

Copyright © 2017 Clyde Winters

All rights reserved.

DEDICATION

This book is dedicated to my students. They were responsible for my many efforts to provide them with a great education.

Contents

DEDICATION iii

List of Tables 6

Preface 7

Chapter 1: Introduction 9

Chapter 2: Central Nervous System and Learning 21

REGIONS REPRESENT STM 41

Chapter 3: Brain research and Learning 42

Chapter 4: Education and the Brain: Closing the Gap 48

Chapter 5: Cognitivism and Brain based Learning 65

Chapter 6: Best Teaching Methods for LD Students 73

Best Teaching Methods for LD Students 87

Character Education 104

Suggested Teaching Strategies 110

Chapter 7: Common Core State Standards and Students with Disabilities 126

Final Word 135

Resources: 144

REFERENCES 145

ABOUT THE AUTHOR 170

List of Tables

FIGURE 1:1. SOCIAL ENVIRONMENT OF BRAIN BASED LEARNING   14

FIGURE 2:1. LEARNING   35

FIGURE 3:1. NEUROBIOLOGICAL LEARNING   41

FIGURE 6:1. BRAIN BASED LEARNING   69

FIGURE 6:2. MECHANISM FOR BRAIN BASED LEARNING   102

FIGURE 6:3. READING TECHNIQUES BASED ON BRAIN RESEARCH   111

FIGURE 6:4. BRAIN BASED MATH TEACHING TECHNIQUES   115

FIGURE 7.1. CONCEPT MAP FOR BRAIN BASED LEARNING   118

Preface

In 1990 while teaching Social Studies at a local High School in Chicago I became aware of the fact that students were entering my classroom unable to read. In an attempt to make my instruction more effective I decided to take a class at Chicago State University in Special Education.

This was the best thing I could have done because, I was introduced to the world of brain based learning by Dr. Angel Diaz. Dr. Diaz had a tremendous influence on my views toward cognitive learning. He taught me the belief that given the right learning/teaching strategy any student can learn.

Over the years teaching pre-service teachers and experienced teachers in seminars and conferences around the nation and at Governors State University and Saint Xavier University-Chicago , I have discovered that many members of the teaching profession are very interested in brain based learning and teaching. In this book I have attempted to explain the role brain based learning can play in the education of students with special needs. This book is written to help teachers learn the most effective and efficient techniques we can use to teach students generally, and special needs students in particular.

Chapter 1: Introduction

It is no secret that many students have been turned off to school and learning because many learning environments fail to provide students with learning opportunities that allow them to create their own meanings of the knowledge they learn. These students find rote memorization and direct instructional methods used in many traditional classrooms boring and uninspiring. To remedy this boredom some educators have begun to introduce brain based teaching and learning to their classrooms, where students create their own knowledge individually, and through collaborative interaction.

More and more teachers are becoming interested in brain based learning. Although there is immense interest among some teachers in brain based learning we have been cautioned by Dr. John Bruer that it may be too early to apply neuroscientific research to teaching. Dr. Bruer (1997) confidently argues that since we know very little about brain development, due to the fact that much of this research has been conducted using non-human subjects, it may not be fully transferable to human beings. Consequently, Bruer (1997) advocates the view that early education is best served by the application of cognitive teaching practices to classroom teaching, rather than neurobiological functioning.

Eventhough Dr. Bruer (1997) argues that neuroscience has "little to offer education", thousands of teachers and school administrators are spending thousands of dollars each year to attend national conferences like the Learning & the Brain Conference sponsored by the National Institute of Mental Health, Kosik Laboratory of Neurobiology (Harvard School of Medicine) and the Public Information Resources group) on brain based learning. And at just about every national conference in the area of education we find at least one paper on brain based learning presented on this topic.

After attending these meetings on brain based learning, teachers are returning to their schools and using brain based teaching methods in their classroom. And, in some school districts around the Nation, entire schools like the Valley Park Elementary School in Kansas City, Kansas have made brain based teaching a central part of their curriculum and method of instruction.

This has made interest in brain based learning skyrocket among teachers. And as a result some administrators at teaching colleges throughout the United States like Chicago State University, are advising their education faculty to investigate the issues related to brain based learning to determine their relevance for use in education courses.

Brain Based learning is based on the structure and function of the brain as an information processor; an entity that has plasticity and can change as a result of purposeful learning ,in classrooms that promotes cognitive learning strategies. It recognizes that practice promotes strengthening learning experiences from the environment so they can be matched with prior learning experiences to produce new knowledge..

Brain based teaching employ's cognitive teaching methods. These teaching methods based on the research of Dr. Jerome Bruner and Dr. Lev Vygotsky demand that students actively construct their own knowledge, until recently were rarely used in the classroom. Many regular education teachers failed to use cognitive teaching strategies, because most teachers favored direct instructional methods which demanded that the teacher, exclusively structure the learning environment and the products resulting from student learning.

Cognitive learning on the otherhand, calls for the constructivist approach to learning advocated by Piaget. This teaching approach calls on the student to construct his or her own knowledge, while obtaining the intellectual and personal competencies which may help them do well in school and in life.

Caine and Caine (1994) maintains that teachers must acknowledge 12 principles in relation to brain based learning. These principles are:

1. The brain is a complex adaptive system that can perform several activities at once.
2. The brain is a social brain .
3. The search for meaning is innate.
4. The search for meaning occurs through patterning.
5. Emotions are critical to patterning.
6. Every brain simultaneously perceives and creates parts and wholes.
7. Learning always involves conscious and unconscious processes.
8. Learning involves both focused attention and peripheral attention.
9. We have at least two ways of organizing memory.
10. Learning is developmental.
11. Complex learning is enhanced by challenge and inhibited by threat.
12. Every brain is uniquely organized.

This means that in brain based learning the learner plays an active role is his or her own learning and construction of knowledge as s/he seeks meaning for his experiences. The learner is active in his learning because s/he customizes their brain based on their personal interactions with the environment.

Brain based teaching is making cognitive learning strategies such as cooperative learning, problem based learning and project based learning more popular among regular education teachers as they seek to encourage students to construct their own knowledge, while they learn information that will help then meet the learning standards the numerous states have developed to enrich the learning of all American children. These teachers demand that their students work in collaborative learning activities that encourage them to create self-knowledge and autonomy through interaction with the teacher and their peers. These learning activities seek to promote higher order thinking skills concurrently with students producing their own knowledge in an environment that values exploration.

In the brain based classrooms appearing throughout the nation educators are supporting:

- Contructivists models for learning and teaching
- Student engagement and active involvement in their own learning;
- Teachers teaching for meaning and understanding rather than rote memorization;
- Teachers creating classroom environments that are low in threat, yet high in challenge
- Teachers immersing their students in complex learning experiences
- Teachers using research to inform instructional practice.

These teaching methods and practices are introducing challenging learning tasks into many classrooms. The evidence multidisciplinary tasks being implemented in classrooms where teachers employ brain based (cognitive) teaching methods and activities that require students to use critical thinking skills while they learn and construct or co-construct their own knowledge.

In the brain based classrooms we witness students engaged in learning activities that create a problem solving learning environment where students work individually or in groups. In this learning environment students make detailed plans, prepare portfolios relating to problem-based projects, demonstrations, artwork and oral presentations. Here we also see students create/formulate their own questions, assisted by teachers working as facilitators or coaches, which they answer themselves. We must acknowledge that this type of teaching reinvigorates many teachers, who for the first time see their children excited about learning.

The research suggest that teachers may find some brain based teaching methods very useful additions to their teaching repertoire because research related to the cognitive teaching methods used by brain based teachers, maximize the learning of many students. Moreover, the fact that many neurosciecientists and teachers have been able to find a common ground between teaching and the findings of neuroscientific research indicate that teachers have the power to judge what, and how research should be applied to their classrooms.

It should be recognized that there are some limitations to brain based learning. First, the cognitive teaching strategy used in a classroom may be inappropriate for the student(s) attempting to use it. Secondly, the emotional makeup of some students may not allow them to work cooperatively in groups, and may lead them to feel incapable of learning. Yet, the fact that cognitive teaching methods can help students learn more efficiently suggest that more teachers should investigate this area and determine for themselves if brain based teaching can help them encourage their students to learn more effectively what they need to know; while embedding within students a desire to be life long learners capable of using critical thinking skills to solve the new and dynamic problems they will meet as members of the work force of the 21st century.

Today Brain based teaching is very popular among many early educators (Wolfe & Brandt,1998). Although this educational idea is popular among some early educators, neuroscientists believe that it is too early to apply cognitive neuroscience to teaching (Bruer, 1997, 1998,1998b). Other researchers such as Hansan and Monk (2002) present research that suggest a close link between neuroscience and learning.

Educators who advocate brain based teaching cast their instructional practice around cognitive teaching methods, based on the findings of neuroscience (Brandt,1997; Calvin,1996; Diaz, 1992; Pool, 1998; Sylvester,1995; Winters, 1994; Wolfe & Brandt, 1998). These researchers believe that they are justified in their educational ideas based on the plasticity of the brain; evidence IQ can be influenced by environmental factors; children can learn best during sensitive periods of the brain; emotion can influence learning; and MRI research findings (Bruer, 1997; Diaz, 1992; Jones,1995; Shaywitz,1996; Sylvester, 1995; Viadero,1996; Winters, 1994,1995; Wolfe & Brandt,1998).

Plasticity of Brain

- Plasticity of the brain encourages the growth of synapses when learning takes place.
- Learning takes place as new connections or synapses are made between brain cells.
- New synapses indicate learning has taken place.
- Failure to use a particular learned behavior weakens a group of synapses and the learned experience may disappear.
- Functions not properly developed or destroyed by brain injury, function is taken over by other cortical area.

Brain based researchers believe that by applying the research findings regarding the role of the brain in learning educators can influence early education practice (Wolfe & Brandt, 1998). They focus their interest on early education because of the rapid development of synapses during the early years. Using this knowledge, brain based teachers hope to develop learning experiences and an enriched environment that can stimulate synaptic growth (Brandt,1997; Calvin, 1996; Cardellichio & Field, 1997; Caine & Caine,1997; Sylvester,1995).

Although we see tremendous interest in brain based education among teachers, there is presently no research base on the application of brain -based learning in the classroom. As a result, much of what we hear is anecdotal. The meager research base for brain based learning makes it clear that we need to know if this method of learning is just an educational fad, or is it a teaching method that has great promise in enhancing the academic achievement of students across the nation.

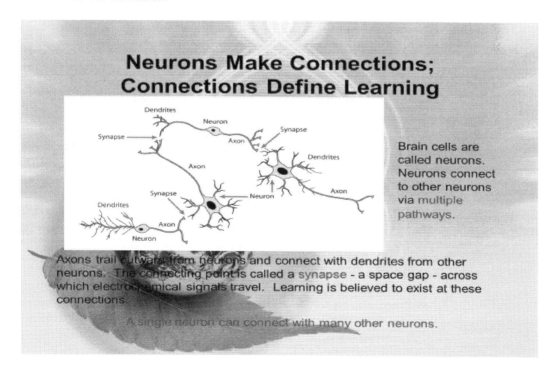

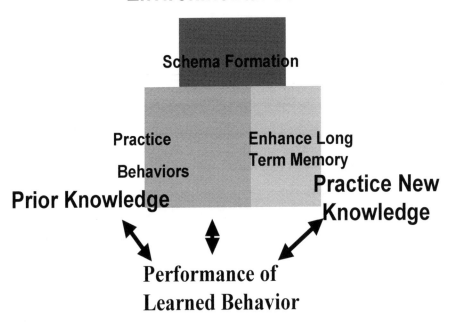

Figure 1.1: <u>**Social Environment of Brain Based Learning**</u>

In this book we will explore the brain based learning phenomena. Here you will find information on how the brain learns and the role cognitivism plays in brain based learning. Finally, this book will seek to explain the research that suggest that brain based learning may be an appropriate method of learning for students with special needs.

Chapter 2: Central Nervous System and Learning

The second largest category in special education is learning disabled (Winters 1994; Ysseldyke, Algozzine & Thurlow 1992). Nationally 43.6 percent of the special education categories served in the United States are students with a learning disability (Ysseldyke, Algozzine & Thurlow 1992).

The presence of a learning disability (LD) implies a processing problem in the central nervous system (CSN) (Diaz 1992; Myers & Hammill 1990; Rothstein & Crosby 1989). This presumes that there is a neurological basis to learning disabilities (Johnson & Myklebust 1967; Winters 1994; Bigler 1990, 1992).

<u>Neurobiological basis of Learning Disability</u>

The National Joint Committee on Learning Disability (NJCLD) makes it clear that this disability is neurologically based. The JCLD defined a learning disability as "intrinsic to the individual presumed to be due to CNS dysfunction, and may occur across the life span "(NJCLD 1989).

A specific LD is not a developmental lag that will be out grown, it is a specific academic or nonverbal learning disability that deserves remediation (Strange & Rourke 1985; Bigler 1990; Silver 1990; Winters 1994). These problems are the result of problems in the neurologic subsystems that coordinate learning. Silver (1990, 397) observed that a learning disability is a neurologically based disorder that interferes with necessary psychological processes need to learn".

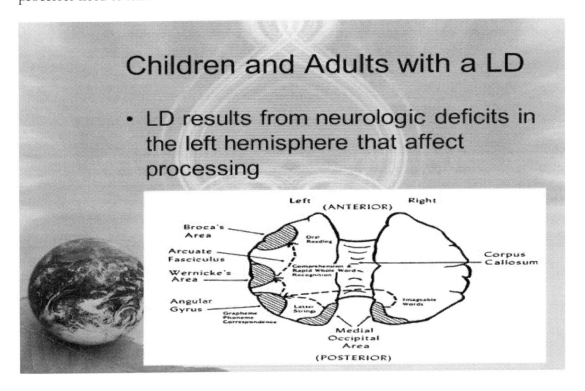

Although many educators accept this definition of LD these specialists know very little about neurobiological learning and the neurological basis of LD. Neurobiological learning can be defined as the neuroanatomical changes that occur in the CSN when an individual accumulates new experiences (Winters 1994; Diaz 1992). Neurobiological learning is modulated by the biological activities of the nervous system.

There is considerable research findings which indicate that LD is the result of neurologic deficits that affect information processing. Dyslexia provides us with a clear example of the neurological basis of a learning disability. Bigler (1992) provides clear explanation of the pathophysiologic basis of dyslexia.

Learning disabilities are primarily neurologic impairment of the left hemisphere (Hooper, Hind & Tramontana 1988; Myklebust 1975; Branch, Cohen & Hynd 1995; Bonnet 1989). The children and adults suffering a learning disability have problems the rehearsal or organization of information (Bauer 1979). They have deficits in visual-spatial functioning (Shafrir & Siegel 1994; Siegel & Linder 1984; Fletcher 1985).

Children and adults have a number of memory deficits. They present problems both in short-term and working memory (Swanson 1994; Shafrir & Siegel 1994; Bauer 1979; Hume 1992).

Children and adults with a LD may present a number of problems
- Have problems in the rehearsal or organization of information
- Deficits in visual-spatial functioning
- Deficits in both short-term and long-term memory

In the case of specific academic learning disabilities children with a learning disability present a series of problems. Research indicate that children with a reading disability suffer from dysfunction in the left hemispheric parietal-temporal cortical areas (Rourke 1985; Rourke, Bakker, Fisk & Strange 1983). And children with arithematic learning disabilities present difficulties with eye-hand coordination, short term memory problems and learning time tables.

Everyday researchers are making it clear that scientific findings by neuroscientists can inform learning and teaching (Brandt,1997;Caine & Caine,1997; Cardellichichio & Field, 1997; Winters, 1994,1996). Brain research is making it clear that the constructivists classroom can be beneficial to the learning of children.

Neuroscientist have made fantastic discoveries about the brain that can inform education. We know now that due to environmental stimuli or mental representations (resulting from the sounds, and sights we experience) the brain is reorganized as neural pathways branch out (Cardellichio & Field,1997). This means that the learning environment customizes our brain.

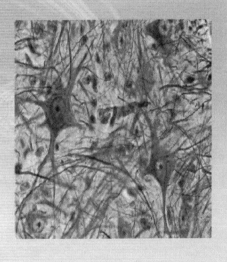

Brain facts that can influence Learning

- The brain is nourished by novelty and repetition
- The learning environment promotes learning and stimulation of many centers of the brain
- The Brain learns best when more than one sense modality is used when they learn .
- As a result, a multisensory learning environment offers the best environment for learning to take place.

The brain is made up of millions of neurons. These neurons transmit, analyze, receive and coordinate information. What the brain can or can not do depends on the use and stimulation of brain cells (Brandt, 1997; Kosslyn & Koenig, 1995; Winters,1994).

Relationship of brain Anatomy and Learning

There are molecular nechanisms that underlie any mental process (Kandel & Hawkins 1992). As a result, learning causes structural changes in the brain. Each learned experience causes connections between brain cells called synapses. To gain an understanding of neurobiological learning we must review the normal anatomy of the brain(Rothstein & Crosby 1989).

Everyday we are learning more and more about the brains anatomy and learning (Rothstein & Crosby 1989; Grady 1984). This knowledge of brain behavior correlates can help us to better understand the role manipulatives can play in the remediation of many problems associated with math.

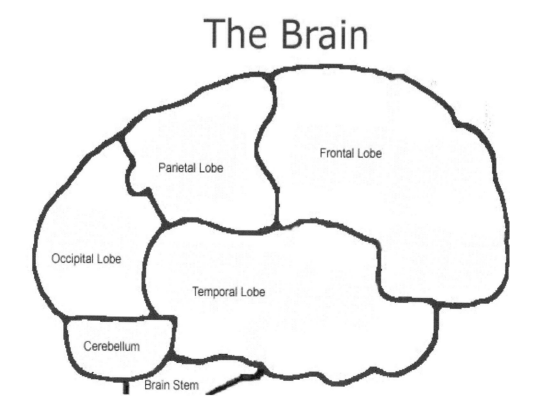

The brain is composed of four layers the spinal cord, cerebral cortex, the hippocampus and thalamus. The cerebral cortex is the outer or wrinkled layer of gray matter neurons or nerve cells making up the brain.

The cerebral cortex is divided into two hemispheres. Each hemisphere has four lobes: the frontal, parietal, occipital and temporal.

The occipital lobe processes visual information. The **primary visual cortex** interprets the raw information. The **secondary visual cortex** recognizes (remembers) that something has a particular purpose or meaning.

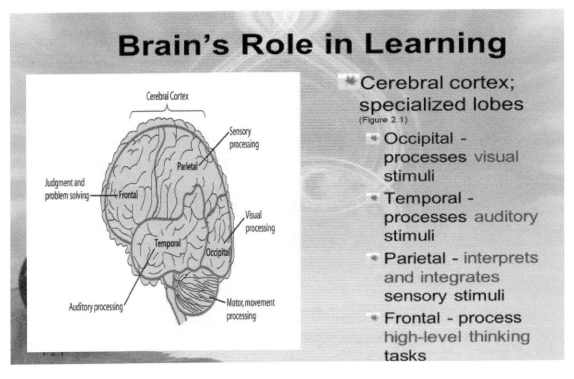

Visual perception and visual imagery activates the primary visual cortex (Miyashito 1995)The occipital lobe processes the visual information and sends it out to other parts of the brain for interpretation.

The processing of cognitive information takes place in the temporal and parietal lobes during different mental activities (Miyashito 1995). The temporal lobe processes auditory information. This lobe names objects, people and animals. The **primary auditory cortex** interprets the raw auditory information.

The **secondary auditory cortex**, recognizes (remembers) that something has a particular purpose or meaning. In general the temporal lobe discriminates between general experiences. Many brain-behavior activities associated with doing cognitive activities are coordinated in the temporal lobe.

The Parietal lobe processes tactile-kinesthetic information. The right **parietal cortex** plays an important role in self-awareness and visual-spatial processing. The parietal lobe and the occipital lobes are mainly used to process information.

The prefrontal lobe is important in many cognitive activities. In this region visual and spatial working memory is carried out (Goldman-Rakic 1992). This region is critical as an intermediary between action and memory. It has multiple memory domains specialized in encoding different information including color, shape and size; and mathematical and semantic knowledge.

The frontal cortex is a very important part of the brain it houses memory and language centers. In the prefrontal cortex decisions are made about what to do or planning things. In this area verbs are processed. Problems in this area would affect a student's ability to pay attention.

The hippocampus is situated on both sides of the brain in the temporal lobe, it is shaped like a finger. In the hippocampus learned memory is controled, episodic and long-term memory is established. They are conveyed from this region to the neocortex (Crick 1994, 83).

A ball shaped object called the thalamus is located in the middle of the head. The thalamus is primarily involved in attentional mechanisms (Crick 1994, 251).

The perisylvian region and basal ganglia are also important in learning. The left basal ganglia, for example, assembles word forms and controls systems for cognitive abilities and movement. The perisylvian region establishes auditory, kinesthetic and motor correspondences for phonemes.

Research indicates that the brain is like a super-sponge. In the brain learning takes place as new connections or synapses are made between brain cells. New synapses indicate learning has taken place. Failure to use a particular skill weakens a group of synapses and the learned experience may disappear.

Two important findings of neuroscience that can inform constructivist education are the plasticity of the brain and role of emotion in learning. Localization of behavior in the brain is not as distinct as scientists formerly believed.

Multiple cortical areas often play important roles in most behaviors. Plasticity of the brain encourages the growth of synapses when learning takes place. As a result, when functions are not properly developed or destroyed by brain injury other cortical areas take over that function.

Neuroscience has also shown that emotion can play an important role in learning (Brandt,1997; Kosslyn & Koenig, 1995). This research indicates that the emotionality of an experience can positively affect long term memory (LTM). This means that when information has emotionality there is greater recall and retention of the learned experience.

Brain research make it clear that children learn best when more than one sense modality is used when they learn (Winters, 1994). As a result, a multisensory learning environment offers the best environment for learning to take place.

The constructivist classroom satisfies this requirement. It meets this goal because it is a classroom where children are engaged in learning activities in which they play a direct role in their own learning. A role in which they work in learning communities to co-construct knowledge using their own hands, eyes, minds and mouths. This compliments the findings of neuroscience that we learn throughout our lifetime, as the brain is transformed by our interaction with the environment. .

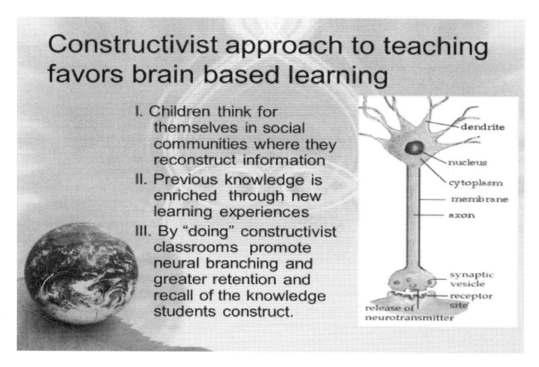

The constructivist classroom provides stimulating learning environment that promotes learning and stimulation of many centers of the brain, which reflects the multiple centers of the brain which carries out many learning experiences. This classroom, because the work is done by the students themselves supports inquiry among children in social learning communities where they co-construct knowledge to create meaning out of their own learning.

The brain is nourished by novelty and repetition (Caine & Caine, 1997; Kosslyn & Koenig, 1997). It is no secret that students in constructivists classrooms usually make hypothesis and pose questions that not only guide their learning, these hypothesis and questions also relate learning to real life. This learning encourages students in the constructivist classroom to use all the senses to perform higher order thinking skills that determine agreed upon solutions to a problem, that promotes neural branching.

As research in cognitive neuroscience became known to the public some special educators also began to recognize that the findings of these researchers might inform educational practice in special education (Diaz,1992; Winters, 1994, 1995). Dr. Angel Diaz, formerly of Chicago State University, was one of the first professional special educators to recognize the possible use of the discoveries of neuroscience in special education instruction.

Dr. Diaz (1992) called this type of instruction: neurobiologic instruction. Neurobiologic instruction can be defined as the use of the neuropsychological knowledge we have of learning disabilities to make our instruction centered toward stimulation of those parts of the brain that moderate behavior/ learning. In this way the teacher can make his instruction more focused toward the specific centers of the brain that can lead to the remediation of the academic deficits exceptional children bring with them to the classroom. Dr. Diaz (1992) has observed that: "Knowledge of the arrangement of the neural networks and the way the individual neuronal processes are connected, how they grow and develop, how their functioning is altered when they do not develop, how they tend to restructure themselves after they have been lesioned or damaged, and how their operation can be modified by dietetic and psychopharmaceutical intake provides a wealth of information from which educators can derive teaching and/ or learning principles. The information can also provide educators with a more appropriate rationale for improving a child's learning efficiency and with improved techniques to identify and remediate learning problems " (p.31).

As shown in the early adoption of cognitive teaching methods to special education, special educators have long been innovators in applying new teaching techniques to special populations. They were inspired to pursue this course by developments in MRI research.

In the 1960's special educators had speculated on the relationship of LD and Dyslexia to brain structure and functioning (Myklebust,1964a,1964b). Developments in MRI made it possible to actually view brain activity while students were carrying out cognitive task (Bruer,1997; Winters ,1994). This provides graphic evidence that during learning specific areas of the brain indicate increased blood flow as a result of cognitive activity.

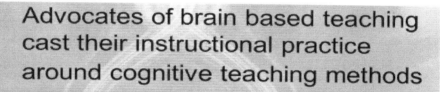

Advocates of brain based teaching cast their instructional practice around cognitive teaching methods

- Based on the plasticity of the brain
- Evidence IQ can be influenced by environmental factors
- Children learn best during sensitive periods of the brain
- Emotion can influence learning
- MRI research findings

Brain Based teaching and Special Populations

There is tremendous interest in applying Brain Based on neurobiological learning in the instruction of students with learning disabilities. Special education has long been an area where innovative teaching techniques have been applied, before they have been adopted by the general education community. For example, ideas such as reciprocal learning, cognitive teaching strategies, metacognition and many other cognitive teaching methods were originally used by special educators (Bruer,1993).

Children with learning disabilities suffer a processing problem (Winters,1994). These problems manifest as academic deficits in reading and math, or attention and memory problems.

Special education teachers in the Public schools are increasingly appreciating the role of neurobiological learning in the instruction of students who are learning disabled. This phenomena is the result of the efforts of Dr. Angel Diaz, a retired professor of Special Education at Chicago State University.

Dr. Diaz in his popular courses on advanced methods in learning disabilities and neurobiological learning has encouraged many special educators to appreciate how the brain's plasticity can be used to help remediate specific academic learning disabilities. The work of Dr. Diaz (1992) is helping children with learning disabilities and Dr. Bigler (1990) in the case of children with Attention Deficit Disorder (ADD).

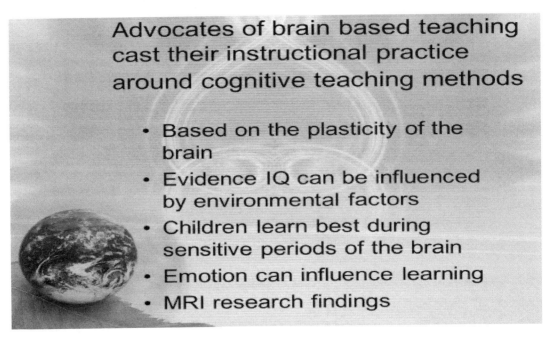

Cognitivism is the view that information individuals obtain and store data that is joined with new data that turns into new types of behavior. Neurobiologic instruction can be defined as the use of the neuropsychological knowledge we have of learning disabilities to make our instruction centered toward stimulation of those parts of the brain that moderate behavior/ learning. This instruction is based upon the principals of learning strategies instruction, neuropsychological testing and task analysis (Winters 1994). In this way the teacher can make his instruction more focused toward the specific centers of the brain that can lead to the remediation of academic deficits exceptional children bring with them to the classroom.

Many researchers have shown that learning disability is neurologically centered (Bigler 1992; Diaz 1992; Silver 1990; Winters 1994). Due to the pathophysiologic bases of many learning problems such as dyslexia (Bigler 1992; Diaz 1992; Winters 1994), we can use our understanding of neurobiologic learning to remediate many learning disabilities (Diaz 1992; Winters 1994).

Many youth and adults have a learning disability. A learning disability is not a developmental lag that will be out grown, it is a specific academic learning disability that deserves remediation (Winters 1994). These learning problems are the result of problems in the neurologic subsystems that coordinate learning.

A person exhibiting a learning disability has a processing problem in the central nervous system. This suggest that learning causes changes in the structure of the brain. The hypothesis that learning causes neuroanatomical changes, that can correct neurologic dysfunctions that are the basis of learning disabilities through the forming of new synapses, has been proven by numerous researchers over the past decade.(Lynch & Baudry 1984; Myers & Hammill 1990; Goldman-Rakic 1992; Bigler 1990)

This brain research makes it possible for learning disabled specialist to use what we know about neuropsychology , special education teaching strategies and learning strategies to affect specific neuroanatomical changes that can help in the remediation of academic deficits and nonverbal problems associated with learning disabilities (Bigler 1990). Bigler (1990)

> "However, as knowledge increased about brain-behavioral relationships, it became evident that the concomitant expression of learning disabilities and problems in social-emotional development shared similar neurologic substrates. This relationship between learning and emotion is a very complex, interactive process. In some cases, a learning disability is a manifestation of a developmental lag in brain maturation which also impedes and slow emotional maturity" (p.321).

Central Nervous System and Learning

To understand how children learn we must have a knowledge of the neural pathways associated with the processing of visual and acoustic information. To learn, children must process information from both of these pathways.

The initial response of the central nervous system to learning are neuroanatomical changes at the synaptic regions in the brain. (Shashoua 1972, 1982) These neuroanatomical changes at the synaptic regions of the brain and receptor sites after a learning experience probably represents short-term (STM) memory. This leads one to speculate that extracellular neurochemicals: proteins and peptides play an important role in the process of long term memory (LTM) or long-term potentiation (LTP) formation, and encoding of the LTM onto the memory trace. As a result, learning requires certain modulating factors that strengthen the memory trace (MT).

This means that learning is a series of memories. A memory occurs when an electrical signal carried by the axon causes a change in the spine. This chemical change encourages postsynaptic LTP that last for months. The LTP is strengthened by repetition and can last indefinitely (Diaz 1992; Lynch & Baudry 1984; Winters 1994).

We argue that because a learning disability has a neurobiological foundation, application of recent findings regarding neurobiological learning can help to remediate many LD problems efficiently. Bigler (1990) has demonstrated the positive application of neurobiological learning theory to the remediation of many non-verbal learning disabilities. Diaz (1992) is also working on cognitive teaching approaches that can positively affect the ability of individuals with learning disabilities to learn especially the use of "emotional teaching" experiences to facilitate strengthening of LTP (Diaz 1992, pp. 135-136).

Research indicates that children with a reading disability suffer from dysfunction in the left hemispheric parietal-temporal cortical areas (Rourke 1985; Rourke, Bakker, Fisk & Strange 1983). Reading problems do not have to always remain forever because neurological research indicates that new synapses can be formed through learning. As a result, many individuals that lose selected neuropsychological functions can recover (Bach-Y-Rita, 1990).

To understand how children learn we must have a knowledge of the neural pathways associated with the processing of visual and acoustic information. To learn, children must process information from both of these pathways.

The initial response of the central nervous system to learning are neuroanatomical changes at the synaptic regions in the brain (Shashoua 1972, 1982). These neuroanatomical changes at the synaptic regions of the brain and receptor sites after a learning experience probably represents short-term (STM) memory. This leads one to speculate that extracellular neurochemicals: proteins and peptides play an important role in the process of long term memory (LTM) or long-term potentiation (LTP) formation, and encoding of the LTM onto the memory trace. As a result, learning requires certain modulating factors that strengthen the memory trace (MT).

This means that learning is a series of memories. A memory occurs when an electrical signal carried by the axon causes a change in the spine. This chemical change encourages postsynaptic LTP that last for months. The LTP is strengthened by repetition and can last indefinitely (Diaz 1992; Lynch & Baudry 1984; Winters 1994).

Research indicates that children with a reading disability suffer from dysfunction in the left hemispheric parietal-temporal cortical areas (Rourke 1985; Rourke, Bakker, Fisk & Strange 1983). Reading problems do not have to always remain forever because neurological research indicates that new synapses can be formed through learning. As a result, many individuals that lose selected neuropsychological functions can recover (Bach-Y-Rita, 1990).

There is considerable research findings which indicate that LD is the result of neurologic deficits that affect information processing. Silver (1990, 397) observed that a learning disability is a neurologically based disorder that interferes with necessary psychological processes need to learn".

The children and adults suffering a learning disability have problems the rehearsal or organization of information (Bauer 1979). They have deficits in visual-spatial functioning (Shafrir & Siegel 1994; Siegel & Linder 1984; Fletcher 1985).Children and adults have a number of memory deficits. They present problems both in short-term and working memory (Swanson 1994; Shafrir & Siegel 1994; Bauer 1979; Hume 1992).

Slowly, psychology is being grounded in biology (Mukerjee 1995. For example, researchers have found a clear association between brain changes in the hippocampus as a result of extreme sexual abuse and long term disturbances of the psyche , including dissociation and post traumatic stress disorder.

To summarize this section Special educators have varying objectives in using brain based teaching methods. The regular educator has one principal objective in using brain based teaching: stimulation of the learners brain (Bruer,1997).The special educator does not seek to only increase stimulation of the brain, s/he seeks to make the student with a learning difficulty a more efficient and capable learning. They therefore use neuropsychology and cognitive neuroscience research to find prescriptions that will remedy (make more manageable)the learning problems of students with a learning difficulty.

Many psychologists believe that neurobiological learning can help make special education instruction more effective. Diaz (1992) and Winters (1994) advocate the use of neurobiological learning data to help remediate learning disabilities. And Bigler (1989,1992) and Riccio and Hynd (1993) have shown the connection between Attention Deficit Disorder and neurobiology.

Figure 2.1: LEARNING

1. LEARNING IS THE PROCESS OF MAKING NEW NEURONS.

2. NEW CONNECTIONS AT SYNAPTIC REGIONS REPRESENT STM

3. PRACTICE MAKES STM INTO LTM THROUGH PRACTICE

4. THE LTMs BECOME A MEMORY TRACE

5. FAILURE TO USE MEMORY LEADS TO ITS LOSS.

6. MEMORIES ARE STORED IN THE HIPPOCAMPUS.

Chapter 3: Brain research and Learning

The foundation of cognitive development is the ability of humans to represent the external events mentally (McShane 1991, 121). To learn, we must process visual and auditory in formation.

There are two types of learning incidental and intentional learning. Incidental learning can be defined as learning without instruction. In school we seek from our students intentional learning, which can be defined as learning with instruction. This form of learning requires explicit memories that are located in the temporal lobe (Goldman-Rakic 1992).

Learning is the accumulation of experiences. Hebb (1964) developed a simple model for learning. The Hebbian model makes it clear that the modification of the neuronal connections at the synapses is the process of learning.

Learning takes place through an integrated process of physiological and behavioral activities. These activities are controlled by neurons.

The neurons have four parts: dendrites (the branches of the neuron),soma (the cell body),axon (the structure that goes to the terminal buds) and terminal buds (that part of the neuron which touches new dendrites). The space between the terminal buds and the dendrite is called the synapse. The number of neurons do not grow it is the connections that grow through stimulation.

Learning is a combination of behaviors, nerve cells and associated molecules and memories produced by events (McShane 1991; Kandel & Hawkins 1992; Winters 1994). Each time an individual accumulates new experiences neurons are formed. These cellular mechanisms for learning make evident the neuronal correlate of learning (NCL).

As a result of NCL each brain is individualized due to the individualized nature of human experience, which in turn will construct the neuronal network in each person (Crick 1994). In other words, our experiences mold our brains to reflect the sum total of the experiences and/or related knowledgebase we have learned during our lifetime.

Stored information in the cerbral cortex is encoded representation of the stimulus input (McShane 1991, 94). The environmental input represents the external world. It becomes a representation in the brain. Crick (1994) defines a representation as "neuronally encoded, structured versions of the world that could potentially guide behavior" (p.66).

Memory

Information for the nervous system comes from transducers. The transducer converts the physical experiences into electrochemical signals (Crick 1994, 82).

In processing information the cognitive system stores information. In the cognitive system stored sensory information is manipulated while the representation of sensory input is stored (McShane 1991, 61). These representations become memories.

Memory development is based on ones "knowlege base". This knowledge base represents the experience one gains from his interaction with his environment (McShane 1991, 163).

Today neuroscientists theorize that there are two memory systems identified as habit and cognitive. The habit system is a group of behaviors that exist as a result of "habit". The cognitive or declarative/ explicit system is made up of "stored representations of stimuli" that are retrieved (Fox 1983).

Atkinson and Shiffrin (1968) theorized that the human cognitive system has three memory storage areas: a sensory register, a short-term store and a long term store. Baddeley and Hatch (1974) believes that we should replace the idea of long and short term stores, with a single memory store which can be activated to process information. According to this cognitive model when part of permenant memory store is activated it becomes "working memory". In the Baddeley and Hatch model for memory working memory functions the same as short-term memory.

Tulving (1972) has made a distinction within the long term memory store between semantic memory and episodic memory. The memory of one's personal experiences and their temporal relations is episodic memory. Semantic memory is one's memory for facts and concepts that transcend individual experience.

Today scientist usually agree on the presence of two memory systems in humans: short-term (STM) and long-term (LTM). These memory systems have submemory systems which include associative and working memory (Baddeley 1990).

To become literate children and adults must be able to access associative and working memory. Working memory can be defined as the simultaneous processing, including recalling and storage of information. A person employs working memory when they must hold a limited amount of data in mind for a limited time while they simultaneously complete further cognitive activities.

Associative memory is the result of facts and figures held in long-term storage, that are retrieved for current use. Working memory is short term memory used to carry out the manipulation of symbolic information without requiring access to associative memory (Goldman-Rakic 1992).

The initial response of the central nervous system to learning are neuroanatomical changes at the synaptic regions in the brain (Shashoua 1982; Thompson 1986). These neuroanatomical changes at the synaptic regions of the brain and receptor sites after a learning experience probably represents short-term (STM) memory. This leads one to speculate that extracellular neurochemicals: proteins and peptides play an important role in the process of long term memory (LTM) or long-term potentiation (LTP) formation, and encoding of the LTM onto the memory trace. As a result, learning requires certain modulating factors that strengthen the MT (Lynch & Baudry 1984; McKean 1983).

In conclusion, learning is a series of memories. A memory occurs when an electrical signal carried by the axon causes a change in the spine. This chemical change encourages postsynaptic LTP that last for months. The LTP is strengthened by repetition and can last indefinitely (Lynch & Baudry 1984).

The plasticity of the brain, which allows corollary brain systems to form new neural pathways indicate that "repetitive treatment strategies" can help people improve CNS functions. The research makes it clear that successful learning occurs when the learner has multiple opportunities to practice a new experience/ behavior the learner is in the process of learning.

Figure 3.1: <u>NEUROBIOLOGICAL LEARNING</u>

1. LEARNING IS NEUROANATOMICAL CHANGES AT SYNAPTIC REGIONS

2. EARLY CHANGES AT SYNAPTIC REGIONS AND BRAIN RECEPTORS SHORT TERM MEMORIES (STMs)

3. STRENGTHENING OF STMs THROUGH REPETITION OF EXPERIENCES ARE LONG TERM MEMORY (LTM)

4. CHANGES AT THE NERVE CIRCUITS REPRESENT ENCODING OF THE LTMs ON THE MEMORY TRACE (MT)

5. LTMs ARE STORED IN THE HIPPOCAMPUS

6. MEMORIES COORDINATED BY PREFRONTAL LOBE

Chapter 4: Education and the Brain: Closing the Gap

Bruer (1997,1998) argues confidently that we cannot build a bridge between neuroscience and early education. He maintains that at this time early education is best served by the application of cognitive teaching practices in the classroom rather than neurobiological findings (Bruer, 1997,1998, 1998b).

Bruer (1997) presents two principal arguments why he believes that neuroscience has "little to offer education" (p.4). Firstly, he argues that we know very little about brain development due to the fact that much of this research has been conducted using non-human subjects and therefore may not be fully transferable to human beings (Bruer, 1997, 1998).

Consequently, Bruer (1997) advocates the view that early education is best served by the application of cognitive teaching practices to classroom teaching, rather than neurobiological functioning.

Secondly, Bruer (1997) argues that neuroscientists do not have enough information between neural functioning and instructional practice. As a result, we can not make a number of claims (made by brain based educators) concerning instructional practices such as a critical learning period for humans, the role of enriched learning environments in early learning, and educational methods that stimulate synaptic growth (Bruer, 1997,1998a, 1999).

Bruer (1999) has modified his views toward brain-based education since 1997. Although he continues to maintain that the idea that critical periods for learning exist among humans is groundless, he has found many positive educational concepts associated with brain-based education.

Bruer (1999) has outlined a number of positive attributes of brain-based education. Bruer (1999) supports some aspects of brain-based education because these educators support:

- Contructivists models for learning and teaching
- Student engagement and active involvement in their own learning;
- Teachers teaching for meaning and understanding;
- Rather than rote memorization;
- Teachers creating classroom environments that are low in threat, yet high in challenge
- Teachers immersing their students in complex learning experiences
- Teachers using research to inform instructional practice;
- Teachers have the power to judge what, and how research should be applied to their classrooms (Bruer, 1999).

The modification of Bruer's (1999) criticism of brain-based education provides considerable support to the possibility that brain based education may be more than an education fad.

Prior to Bruer's (1999) modification of his views regarding brain-based education, Bruer (1997) recognized that if brain based education had any ability to radically change educational practice and instruction, it would first be applied to special education. Bruer (1997) noted that:

> When we do begin to understand how to apply
>
> cognitive neuroscience in instructional context, it
>
> is likely that it will first be of most help in
>
> addressing the educational needs of special
>
> populations (p.14).

This statement is valid, because many special educators early applied the first cognitive theories of educational practice in the special education classroom (Bruer, 1997; McPhail & Palincsar, 1998; Moats & Lyon, 1993; Polloway & Patton, 1989). As a result it is only natural that he would assume that special educators would also find the findings of cognitive neuroscience to be applicable to teaching people with a learning disability.

In the 1960's special educators had speculated on the relationship of LD and Dyslexia to brain structure and functioning (Myklebust,1964a,1964b). Developments in MRI made it possible to actually view brain activity while students were carrying out cognitive task (Bruer,1997; Diaz,1992; Jones,1995; Shaywitz, 1996; Viadero, 1996; Winters ,1994). This process provides graphic evidence that during learning specific areas of the brain indicate incrased blood flow as a result of cognitive activity.

Brain imaging research has helped us to attain a greater understanding of the psychoneurological foundation of LD processing problems (McPhail & Palincsar, 1998; Shaywitz, 1997; Shaywitz & Shaywitz, 1996). For example, in the area of reading MRI's have made it clear that many students with a learning disability are experiencing phonological processing problems (Shawitz & Shawitz, 1996). This finding supported the earlier research into the reading processing problems of children with learning disabilities resulting from neuropsychological testing of these children in the 1970's (Fletcher, *et al.*, 1974; Lieberman, *et al.*, 1974).

To summarize this section Special educators have varying objectives in using brain based teaching methods. The regular educator has one principal objective in using brain based teaching: stimulation of the learners brain (Bruer,1997).The special educator does not seek to only increase stimulation of the brain, s/he seeks to make the student with a learning difficulty a more efficient and capable learning. They therefore use neuropsychology and cognitive neuroscience research to find prescriptions that will remedy (make more manageable)the learning problems of students with a learning difficulty.

Neurobiological basis of Learning Disability

Educational neuropsychology can help us understand the role of the brain in academic functionalism (Diaz,1992; Myklebust, 1964). Educational neuropsychology examines the learner's interconnected brain systems to determine the locus of dysfunction, and make remediation decisions (Berninger, 1996).

A specific LD is not a developmental lag that an individual will out grow, it is a specific academic or nonverbal learning disability that requires remediation (Learner, 1988; Strang & Rourke 1985; Bigler 1990; Silver 1990; Winters 1994). These problems are the result of problems in the neurologic subsystems that coordinate learning. Silver (1990) observed that a "learning disability is a neurologically based disorder that interferes with necessary psychological processes need to learn" (p.397).

> **Learning Disabilities and Brain Based Learning (BBL)**
> - BBL works best among students with learning disabilities
> - A LD is not developmental lag
> - A LD is a specific academic or nonverbal learning disability that deserves remediation
> - A LD is a neurological "disorder that interferes with necessary psychological processes needed to learn "

Although many educators accept this definition of LD these specialists know very little about neurobiological learning and the neurological basis of LD (Winters, 1994). Neurobiological learning can be defined as the neuroanatomical changes that occur in the CNS when an individual accumulates new experiences (Winters 1994; Diaz 1992). Neurobiological learning is modulated by the biological activities of the nervous system (Hebb, 1964).

In the case of specific academic learning disabilities children with a LD present a series of problems (Rourke, 1978, 1985; Rourke & Strang, 1984). Children with a math LD usually indicate difficulties with eye-hand coordination and memory deficits (Goldman-Rackic, 1992).

Controversy surrounds the LD and ADHD special education categories. The presence of a learning disability (LD) implies a processing problem that arises from a dysfunction in the central nervous system (CNS) (Diaz 1992; Kolb & Whishaw, 1990; Bonnet, 1989; Myers & Hammill 1990; Rothstein & Crosby 1989; Winters, 1995). This presumes that there is a neurological basis to learning disabilities (Johnson & Myklebust 1967; Winters 1994; Bigler 1990, 1992).

There is considerable research findings which indicate that LD is the result of neurologic deficits that affect information processing. They are divided into several subtypes including verbally mediated learning disabilities (Fisk & Rourke, 1979; Rourke, 1978; Spreen & Haaf, 1986); and overlapping nonverbal neuropsychological processes (Hooper, Hynd & Tramontana, 1988; Myklebust, 1975; Rourke & Strang, 1984). These learning disabilities can result from problems in either the right cerebral hemisphere (Hooper, Hynd & Tramontana, 1995; Branch, Cohen & Hynd, 1995; Bonnet, 1989; Hulme, 1992) or the left cerebral hemisphere (Rourke, 1985; Rourke, Bakker, Fisk & Strang, 1983) of the brain.

The person affected by a learning disability can have many memory problems, both in short-term and working memory (Swanson, 1994; Shafrir & Siegel, 1994; Hume, 1992). In addition, some children and adults suffering a learning disability have problems in the rehearsal or organization of information (Bauer, 1979). Other children and adults can have deficits in visual-spatial functioning (Shafrir & Siegel, 1994).

Math Learning Disabilities

Children with a mathematical disability (MD) have procedural and fact retrieval deficits (Brynes, 2001). As a result students with a procedural deficit usually demonstrate an unsystematic retrieval system for math facts, or recall fewer facts when performing math operations and applications than children who are not diagnosed with a MD. They also make many errors in calculation; lack speed in naming numbers; comparing the various sizes of numbers and speed in processing information due to problems in working memory.

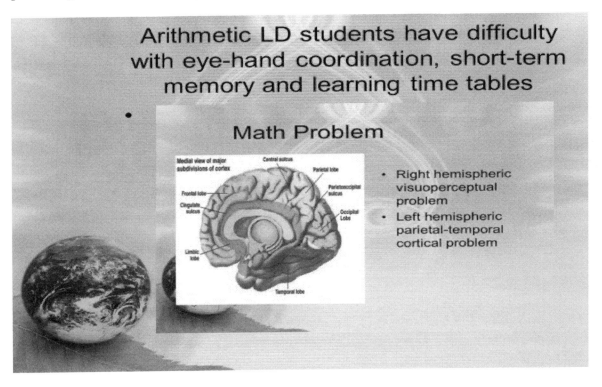

Specific centers of the brain are associated with a math learning disability. In addition to visual-spatial deficits, individuals with a learning disability present neuropsychological deficits in the posterior right hemispheric, and tertiary cortical regions which subserve centers for linguistic analysis and comprehension (Lyons. 1996b; Luria, 1973).

The posterior right hemisphere is associated with deficits in the comprehension and production of word problems. Problems in calculations, conceptualization problem solving and abstract reasoning point to deficiencies in the frontal lobes (Novick & Arnold, 1988).

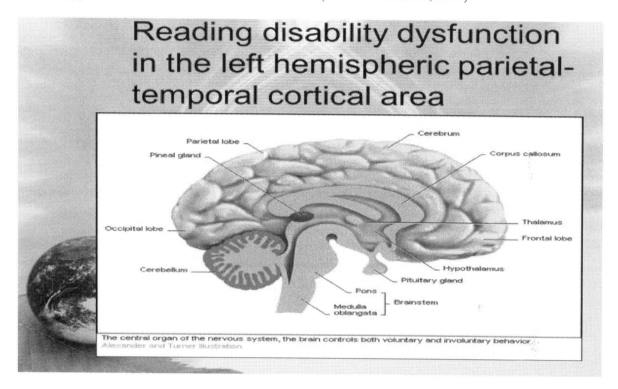

Reading Learning Disabilities

There appears to be an underlying brain mechanism for a learning disability (Winters, 1994; Diaz, 1992; Lyons, 1996b; Shaywitz & Shaywitz, 1996). This is suggested by the functional magnetic resonance imaging which illustrates physiological changes occurring in the brain when it is activated.

The brain processes language in both hemisphere, even though much of the language function takes place in the left hemisphere. The language system has a number of hierarchical components focused on a specific part of language. As a result, discourse, phonological semantics and syntax are processed in distinctive sections of the brain language hierarchy. Thusly, we find that letter identification activates the extra striate cortex in the occipital lobe; while phonological processing activates the inferior frontal gyrus (Broca's area). And the assessing of word meanings takes place in the superior temporal gyrus, middle gyrus and supera marginal gyri (Kolb & Whishaw,1990).

Neuroimaging studies indicate some of the neurobiological deficits associated with a reading disability. It would appear from these studies that individuals with learning disabilities illustrate problems in the left hemisphere associated with the perisylvian fissure, and left temporal region of the brain (Lyons, 1991, 1996a, 1996b). Individuals with a reading learning disability show less activation in the left temporal region; and increased excitation of the angular gyrus (Wood, 1990; Wood, et al, 1991). These biological functions associated with reading are supported by blood flow studies (Lyons, 1996b), positron emission tomography (Gross- Glenn, et al, 1986), and structural magnetic resonance imaging (Filipek & Kenedy, 1991; Lubs, et al, 1991).

Neurobiological research indicates a strong correlation between hemispheric specialization and reading. The left hemisphere processes consonants, while in the right hemisphere we process vowels, detect pitch, intonation, stress, cadence, loudness and softness (Kolb & Whishaw, 1990; Diaz, 1992). In general the left hemisphere is alleged to be dominant for reading comprehension (Kolb & Whishaw, 1990).

Reading learning disabilities provide us with a clear example of the neurobiological basis of a learning disability (Bonnet, 1989; Bigler, 1992, p.490) . Bigler (1992) provides clear explanations of the pathophysiologic basis of dyslexia.

Reading is no longer assumed to be a function totally depended on the left-hemisphere. Reading involves both hemispheres of the brain (Kolb & Whishaw, 1990). Initially the right cerebral hemisphere mediates reading because of the visual-spatial properties necessary for interpretation of alphabetic symbols and written text (Bakker & Licht, 1986; Licht, 1988). Later, the left hemisphere performs the phonological and grammatical analysis, while the right hemisphere extracts semantic information and makes the graphemic analysis (Kolb & Whishaw, 1990, p.799).

Learning obstacles associated with dyslexia include problems in left-hemisphere-mediated behaviors (Bigler, 1989 1992; Kolb & Whishaw, 1990, p. 797) and demonstrated verbal and memory deficits. Among dyslexics a deficit in the phonological component of the language hierarchy fails to segment words into their phonological components (Shaywitz, 1996, 100). Shaywitz (1996) believes that this phonological deficit seems to be the main cause of dyslexia.

Right hemispheric disorders can affect a child's academic performance, because some children have right hemispheric language dominance (Bakker, 1990; Van Strien, Stock & Zuiker, 1995). Moreover, Bakker (1990) found that perceptual dyslexics relied on right-hemispheric visuoperceptual processing and were unable to switch over to the left hemisphere to make semantic interpretations.

Although there is hemispheric specialization, both hemispheres of the brain are involved in reading (Kolb & Whishaw, 1990). Initially the right cerebral hemisphere mediates reading because of the visual-spatial properties necessary for interpretation of alphabetic symbols and written text (Bakker & Licht, 1986; Licht 1988). Later, the left hemisphere performs the phonological and grammatical analysis of the text, while the right hemisphere extracts semantic information and make the graphic analysis (Kolb & Whishaw, 1990, p.799). This makes it clear, that if children and adults with academic learning disabilities hope to function successfully in school situations they must be free of cerebral dysfunction on both sides of the brain.

NEUROPSYCHOLOGICAL

Neuropsychology is the integration of the physiological maturational forces of the brain and psychological development. This has made the **task analytic approach** important in the diagnosis of neuropsychological processing problems. Processing is defined as the way a person understands and retains holistic information.

As a result of this theory professionals working with LD children believe that common learning disabilities are the result of intrinsic neurological impairment. The presence of an LD may not be due to cell damage. But the brain is dysfunctional as a result of the lack of development or damage.

The neurological dysfunction results in problems in academic and developmental processes. These problems are usually "corrected" by professionals seeking out a child's specific skill deficit for remediation.

In learning the student must use both associative and working memory. Patricia S. Goldman-Rakic (1992) noted that "A simple activity involving working memory is the carry-over operation in mental arithmetic, which requires temporarily storing a string of numbers and holding the sum of one addition in mind while calculating the next move". A more complex example, is performing multiplication. In multiplication the student not only has to hold the multiplicand and the multiplier in the working memory, s\he also has to go into the long term memory to retrieve the product. This math knowledge is probably stored in the prefrontal cortex.

Most of the principals in teaching children with a learning disabled person is the neuropsychological approach of Helmer Myklebust. Myklebust (1964b,1968,1975) developed a comprehensive theory of learning disabilities. The neuropsychological teaching approach encourages 1) testing, 2) assessment and 3) diagnosis. Myklebust theorized that the brain was made up of semi-independent systems that either function in an independent or interdependent manner. Basically, you make diagnosis to lead to the treatment of the child's learning problem through a learning prescription.

Myklebust's idea of interrelated systems modulating brain operations led him to develop his concept of interneurosensory learning. Interneurosensory can be defined as learning that "utilizes all these systems to functioning simultaneously". (Johnson & Myklebust 1967, p.26)

Myklebust encouraged the use of psychological testing as a diagnostic tool to discover student weaknesses for remediation. This remediation was to be accomplished by using the student's positive modalities. In general the Myklebust and Johnson (1967) teaching approach encouraged multisensory stimulation for the learner and addresses the student's weaknesses while teaching through the student's strengths.

Some researchers have questioned the frequency of integrative learning. (Myers & Hammill 1991, p.133) Today due to dynamic neurological research we know that integrative learning is the primary model for learning.[i]

According to Johnson and Myklebust (1967) there are several types of learning disabilities:

1) Auditory disabilities,

2) Reading disabilities,

3) Written language disabilities,

4) Arithmetic disabilities, and

5) Non-verbal learning disabilities.

These disabilities result from the lack of three integrities. According to Myklebust (1964b) the integrities necessary for learning are:

1) **Peripheral**- you must be able to see and hear

correctly;

2) **Central Nervous System**- must have good function;

3) **Psychodynamic**- is the psychological dimension

of man (this is based on the

psychological experiences each

person experiences.

Myklebust (1968; Johnson & Mylebust 1967) from this analysis of the learning style of disabled children developed the idea that children should be process analyzed. Students have to be analyzed, i.e., the psychological testing of LD students to determine how they process information. It is necessary to process analyze the child so the instructor can understand the total child, and his acquisition of skills to determine the

child's disability or lack of development.

In summary although there is no clear link between neuroscience and learning, the findings from MRIs provide evidence that during learning experiences, the brain is modified (Hansan & Monk, 2002). The brain is able to be modified due to the neuroplasticity of the brain. . Schwartz and Begley (2002) note that:

"We now know that the circuits of our minds

change when our fingers fly over the strings of a

Brain Based Learning

violin; they change when we suffer an amputation: or a stroke; they change when our ears become tuned to the sounds of our native language and deaf to the phonemes of a foreign one. They change, in short, when the flow of inputs from our senses changes" (p.367).

This evidence make it clear that special educators can teach toward specific areas of the brain to remediate specific learning disabilities of children with special needs.

Chapter 5: Cognitivism and Brain based Learning

Cognition relates to the way we think. It is conditioned links between the conscious, and stored stimuli. As a result, learner expectancy can influence the learner's cognitions.

During cognition we pay attention to new information, that we encode in the long term memory, and later retrieve for elaboration of new knowledge from the environment in association with the individual's prior knowledge. After processing of information via cognition the learner produces a number of cognitive products including decisions, attributions, thoughts and beliefs.

Cognition includes a number of components including cognitive structures like the memory stores; and cognitive positions such as episodic knowledge and semantic knowledge.

Cognitivists view cognition as the processing of encoding meaningful information into the human memory system. To learn the learner should have the following prerequisites: good fine and gross motor movements; good auditory and perceptual ability; discrimination (left/right, up/down); and good attention. Possessing these intact skill prerequisites the learner is able to pull information from the long term memory store into working memory for further processing.`

Brain Based Learning

To understand how information is processed via cognition we use the multistore model. The multistore model for information processing relates to the human memory system which includes the sensory register, short term memory (STM) and long term memory (LTM).

Each memory store has its own purpose. The sensory register is the first port of cognitive processes where information is processed. The STM is that area of memory where information is held until it is used to process new information. The LTM is the permanent storage facility for information. Working memory (WM) stores and holds that information which a person works with. We believe that WM holds seven items of information for a relatively short time for human processing

The memory register becomes aware of the environmental stimuli perceived by the hands, ear or eyes. This register is often referred to as the STM. Here information is made into small bits of meaningful knowledge that is maintained through rehearsal.

Long term memory holds information that can be recalled. This information is enhanced after repetition and practice of the material. Here information experiences elaboration, as the learner links prior knowledge to new information, to make totally new knowledge.

Information in the LTM is elaborated on the macro level and micro level. Macro level elaboration is the method teachers use to help students comprehend the entire lesson. To make elaboration on this level the teacher moves from the general ideas to specific ideas. Teachers using this method provide students information that anchors new information.

Teachers promote microlevel elaboration of long term memories when they provide students with assistance in storing and recalling specific information. In microlevel elaboration, the learner pairs prior knowledge with new information in paired associations.

The LTM includes several memory stores. **Episodic** memory is our memory of time and places. **Semantic** memory is our memories for general facts and concepts (i.e., instructional content). **Procedural memory** is our ability to recall specific skills and concepts used to complete a task.

There are several stages in procedural knowledge used to perform a task. Procedural knowledge is knowing how to do something like riding a bike or tying your shoes. The first stage in PK is the declarative stage. At this stage the learner understands the procedures needed to complete a task. Once a learned behavior or skill is strengthen by active practice, performance of this task will become automatic.

The next stage is the associative stage. At this stage the learner can perform the procedures to complete a task while they think about what they must do.

The third stage in PK is the automatic stage. At this stage the learner performs a task with little conscious thought. The goal of teaching is to guide the student to the automatic stage of procedural knowledge consumption.

Working memory is defined as the simultaneous processing of knowledge by recalling stored information in the LTM. In the WM you hold a limited amount of information in the "mind" for a limited amount of time while simultaneously completing further cognitive activities.

Information obtained by the learner from the environment is transformed in the memory stores to representations or schema. The schemata has many purposes. These purposes include: the human ability to interpret past experiences; the ability to code, discriminate, weigh and screen stimuli; the ability to establish the boundaries for evaluating and judging reality; and the ability to determine the motivations behind selected behaviors.

Cognitivism is the view that information individuals obtain from the environment is joined with new data that turns into new types of behavior. Neurobiologic instruction can be defined as the use of the neuropsychological knowledge we have of learning disabilities to make our instruction centered toward stimulation of those parts of the brain that moderate behavior/ learning. This instruction is based upon the principals of learning strategies instruction, neuropsychological testing and task analysis (Winters 1994). In this way the teacher can make his instruction more focused toward the specific centers of the brain that can lead to the remediation of academic deficits exceptional children bring with them to the classroom.

As research in cognitive neuroscience became known to the education community some special educators recognized that the findings of cognitive researchers might inform educational practice in special education (Diaz,1992; Winters, 1994, 1995). Dr. Angel Diaz, was one of the first professional special educators to recognize the possible use of neuroscience research in special education instruction. Dr. Diaz (1992) called this type of instruction: neurobiologic instruction. Neurobiologic instruction can be defined as the use of the neuropsychological knowledge we have of learning disabilities to make our instruction centered toward stimulation of those parts of the brain that moderate behavior/ learning. In this way the teacher makes his instruction more focused toward the specific centers of the brain that can lead to the remediation of the academic deficits children with special needsbring with them to the classroom. Dr. Diaz (1992) has observed that:

"Knowledge of the arrangement of the neural networks

and the way the individual neuronal processes are connected, how they grow and develop, how their functioning is altered when they do not develop, how they tend to restructure themselves after they have been lesioned or damaged, and how their operation can be modified by dietetic and psychopharmaceutical intake provides a wealth of information from which educators can derive teaching and/ or learning principles. The information can also provide educators with a more appropriate rationale for improving a child's learning efficiency and with improved techniques to identify and remediate learning problems (p.31)."

Brain based teaching employ cognitive learning strategies

- Cooperative learning,
- Problem based learning
- Project based learning
- These strategies encourage students to construct their own knowledge

Brain Based Learning

As shown in the early adoption of cognitive teaching methods to special education, special educators have long been innovators in applying new teaching techniques to special populations. They were inspired to pursue this course by developments in magnetic resonance imaging (MRI) and positron emission topography (PET) and other brain imaging research that has transformed our understanding of the way the brain works. This research has also shown us how learning effects changes in the brain (Shaywitz, 1997, 2003).

Chapter 6: Best Teaching Methods for LD Students

In this era of high stakes testing teachers are interested in finding the best possible teaching practices that can help their students learn. This need for effective teaching techniques to perfect student learning has led to tremendous interest among teachers of applying brain based or neurobiological learning strategies in the instruction of students with learning disabilities. Special education has long been an area where innovative teaching techniques have been applied, before they have been adopted by the general education community. For example, ideas such as reciprocal learning, cognitive teaching strategies, metacognition and many other cognitive teaching methods were originally used by special educators (Bruer,1993). Children with learning disabilities suffer a processing problem (Winters,1994). These problems manifest as academic deficits in reading and math, or attention and memory problems (Winters, 1994,1995, 2000).

The child with a learning disability may have problems in attention; encoding; LTM deficiencies and information retrieval. This means that the learning disabled child usually has lower verbal and visual-spatial scores on test that demand the learner use working memory (Terry, 2003).

Brain Based Learning

Learning requires both associative and working memory. Associative memory is the result of facts and figures held in long-term storage, that are retrieved for current use. Working memory is short term memory used to carry out the manipulation of symbolic information without requiring access to associative memory (Goldman-Rakic 1992).

Learning Reading and Math appears to depend on two reasoning processes: attention and discrimination. You must pay attention to learn (Rothstein & Crosby 1989).

Attention is divided into three types: focusing attention, maintaining attention, and shifting attention. These three types of attention must be intact for learning to take place.

There are two types of learning incidental and intentional learning. Incidental learning can be defined as learning **without** instruction. In school we seek from our students intentional learning, which can be defined as learning **with** instruction. This form of learning requires explicit memories that are located in the temporal lobe.

Cognitivism is the view that information individuals obtain and store data that is joined with new data that turns into new types of behavior. Neurobiologic instruction can be defined as the use of the neuropsychological knowledge we have of learning disabilities to make our instruction centered toward stimulation of those parts of the brain that moderate behavior/ learning. This instruction is based upon the principals of learning strategies instruction, neuropsychological testing and task analysis (Winters 1994). In this way the teacher can make his instruction more focused toward the specific centers of the brain that can lead to the remediation of academic deficits exceptional children bring with them to the classroom.

Many researchers have shown that learning disability is neurologically centered (Bigler 1992; Diaz 1992; Silver 1990; Winters 1994). Due to the pathophysiologic bases of many learning problems such as dyslexia (Bigler 1992; Diaz 1992; Winters 1994), we can use our understanding of neurobiologic learning to remediate many learning disabilities (Diaz 1992; Winters 1994).

Many youth and adults have a learning disability . A learning disability is not a developmental lag that will be out grown, it is a specific academic learning disability that deserves remediation (Winters 1994). These learning problems are the result of problems in the neurologic subsystems that coordinate learning .

A person exhibiting a learning disability has a processing problem in the central nervous system. This suggest that learning causes changes in the structure of the brain. The hypothesis that learning causes neuroanatomical changes , that can correct neurologic dysfunctions that are the basis of learning disabilities through the forming of new synapses, has been proven by numerous researchers over the past decade.(Lynch & Baudry 1984; Myers & Hammill 1990; Goldman-Rakic 1992; Bigler 1990)

Cognitive development is the human capacity to represent mentally objects and events existing in the real world (McShane, 1991, p.121). Wong and Wong (1988) have observed that:

"...the basic tenet in cognitive psychology, namely,

the centrality of the student s' active

participation in and responsibility for the

learning" (p.26).

A cognitive view of learning focuses on changes in mental processes humans use to interpret the world and exploit cognitive structures , or schema. The cognitive view of learning makes it clear that the individual makes sense of the social world by providing it with a concrete base, via concrete experiences based on the experiences we encounter in the world. This schema allow us to represent environmental experiences (actions, people, places and events) that internally change a person's mental structures into new behaviors that demonstrate a different behavior than that previously existed. This intellectual process of internal change of a learner's mental structures that transforms information from one memory store to the next is called cognitive process (STM-> LTM-> WM). As a result, in cognitive learning current learning is built upon prior schemata (units of cognitive structure) or knowledge to make new knowledge.

To organize the knowledge we acquire via interactions with the environment we place that knowledge into two categories declarative knowledge and procedural knowledge. Declarative knowledge is ones knowledge about something, or facts (the ability to "know" something). Examples of declarative knowledge is recognition of the fact that fish swim, or circles are round. Procedural knowledge, is the understanding we have to perform a particular task or skill (knowing "how" to do something).

The cognitive of learning is based on the work of many researchers. For example, cognitivist support their learning theory based on the work of E.C. Tolman. Dr. Tolman introduced the idea of cognitive maps and latent learning. These ideas stressed the fact that human beings organize information so that it is accessible for later use. These ideas along with Tolman's promotion of the idea that we need practice to reinforce our learning supported the view that student learning can be enriched through student active practice of the knowledge they have already learned as the principle way to maintain their knowledge.

Cognitivists have also included the ideas of B.K. Skinner in developing the concept of cognitive learning. These researcher maintain that effective learning is the result of the interaction between a stimulus and response behavior.

As a result, cognitivists believe that as a result of regular practice the learner can perfect knowledge he has or is learning via S-R cognitive mediation to the point that the new learning becomes automatized.

The principle way cognitivist view that this learning can become automatized is by increasing the learner's content knowledge base. A knowledge base that is further extended by the regular practice of this knowledge base by the learner. This means that the primary motive for the learner to learn through cognition is the learner's need to achieve or possess competence in what it is s/he has learned.

This means that the teacher using cognitive methods to teach children with learning disabilities much try to make learning similar to the learners real world experience; and that the learner be provided multiple opportunities for practice of what s/he has learned. This type of learning is facilitated best by providing the learner with knowledge of the prerequisites of what s/he is to learn before the transfer of knowledge actually takes place; and then demonstrate to the learner how s/he can apply the new knowledge themselves so the learner becomes an active constructor of his/her own knowledge.

Cognitive teaching methods used in brain based teaching offer the student with a learning disability the best means to remediate a learning disability, because these teaching strategies can result in changing neural pathways of the learning disabled student, so they can perform learning task they previous were incapable of completing. This change in the brain chemistry is possible because of neuroplasticity, the ability of the brain to restructure itself as a result of mindfulness. Mindfulness or mindful awareness can be defined as the student's mindful notation of the facts, concepts or skills being learned, as s/he is being instructed by the teacher, in order to enhance the mental act of bare attention or focused observation on the lesson or task being taught or model by the instructor.

This is possible by applying a Four Step regimen, when teaching students with a learning disability the learning strategies they need to perform a learning task, that will bring about changes in the way they think about their own ability to learn, which in turn will result in changes in the brain. Learning strategies help students with special needs to apply to their own knowledge and abilities in the acquisition and performance of specific math and reading tasks.

The Four Step regimen for brain based learning is modeled on the Four Steps cognitive therapy method. Dr. Jeffrey M. Schwartz, a professor of psychiatry at the UCLA School of Medicine used the Four Steps method to alter the brain chemistry of obsessive-compulsive disorder patients, so they could lead more normal and productive lives in which they managed OCD (Schwartz and Begley, 2003). Commenting on this regimen, Schwartz and Begley (2003) noted that "The changes the Four Sreps can produce in the brain offered strong evidence that willful, mindful effort can alter brain function and that such self-directed brain changes-neuroplasticity—are a genuine reality. Let me repeat thuis: the Four Steps is not merely a self-therapy; it is also an avenue for self-directed neuroplasticity" (p.94).

Shaywitz Phonological Model

- Use MRI's to identify deficits in brain that may affect Dyslexia
- Determine if student can discriminate different sounds
- Transfer phonemic awareness

The Four Steps are: Relabeling, Reattributing,, Refocusing, Revaluing. The teacher is to help the student to change the way he feels about his disability by providing him with the metacognitive or learning strategy by relabeling, reattributing, refocusing, and revaluing the way they feel about their ability to learn and perform specific academic tasks.

Teaching the student a cognitive learning strategy should allow the student to relabel his attitude about performance of a task. Learning a cognitive strategy will fit the student's perception of what it takes to successfully complete or perform a particular task. This relabeling of the task as one the student can complete, gives the student with special needs frame of reference that allows that student to attribute his academic success to his or her own productivity.

Many students with special needs believe that can not, and will not be able to perform a task. During may years of working with students I have found that many students will swear they can not perform a task, and will even convince themselves, without even trying that the academic task is too difficult. These feelings of learned helplessness can often be eliminated by teaching students specific cognitive learning strategy.

The special needs student's acquisition of a learning strategy to perform academic tasks, leads to their reattributing

Of their ability from an external locus of control to an intrinsic locus of control. In reattributing his ability to perform an academic task, the student with special needs will reject the idea s/he can not perform a task, by telling themselves they can perform the task. This is done by the teacher allowing the special needs students to demonstrate their performance of a task after the teacher models the task for the student.

I have found that the refocusing of the student with a learning disability attitude about his own ability is the direct result of teaching that student a cognitive learning strategy. Refocusing occurs when the student is taught a specific learning strategy because acquisition of the strategy makes it possible for the student to perform new academic tasks. Thus the student refocuses his attention away from passively feeling he will fail in the performance of a task, to carrying out the academic task s/he needs to perform while employing metacognition and the strategy s/he has learned.

Refocusing the student's attitude toward his or her ability to perform a academic task—via employment of the cognitive learning strategy—will change the brain pathways associated with his learning disability. Schwartz and Begley (2003) write that "when patient's changed the focus of their attention, in other words the brain might change, too" (p.85). The research makes it clear that refocusing "strengthens a new automatic circuit and weakens the old pathological one-training the brain, in effect, to replace old bad habits programmed into the caudate nucleus and basal ganglia with healthy new one" (Schwartz & Begley, 2003, p.90).

Many students with special needs want to learn and value their ability to perform academic tasks normally like their peers. This means that we must change the way they value education and their own learning.

Ludwig von Mises, writing in <u>The ultimate foundation of economic science: An essay on method</u> noted that valuing is "man's emotional reaction to various states of his environment, both that of the external world and that of the physiological conditions of his own body".

Students with a learning disability have normal intelligence. This means that most of these students can perform normal tasks, outside the school environment. They just can not perform specific academic tasks. This makes some of these students feel as if they are "dummies".

This means that students with a learning disability must revalue their ability to cope with the demands of learning in the school environment. Learning a cognitive learning strategy allows the student to effectively and efficiently perform academic tasks. Acquisition of the ability to perform a particular learning strategy will encourage the student to revalue his ability to learn. In revaluing his ability to learn, the student realizes that through performance of the steps required in a cognitive learning strategy s/he can use metacognition to affect their own ability to learn and value their extension of their knowledge base.

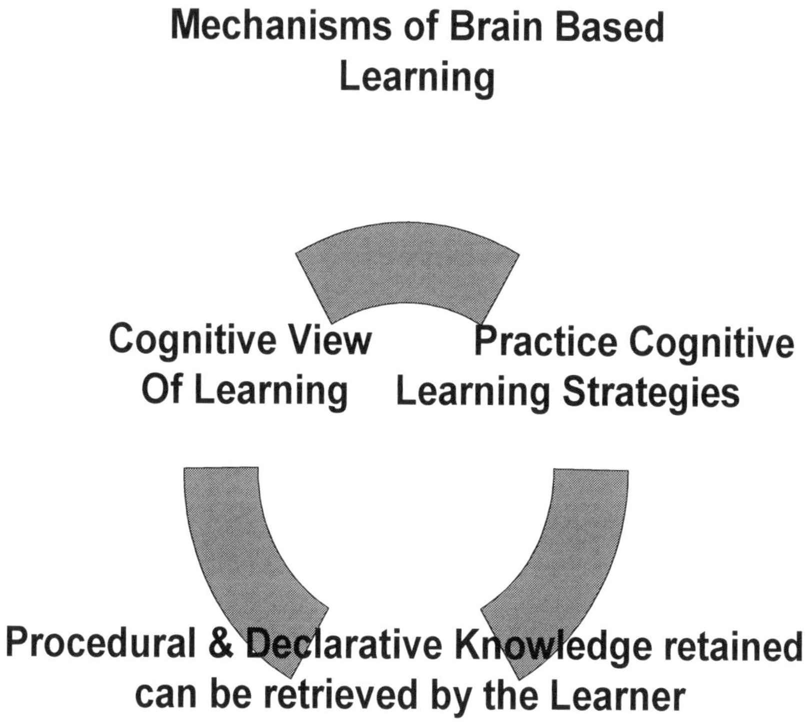

Mechanisms of Brain Based Learning

Cognitive View Of Learning → Practice Cognitive Learning Strategies → Procedural & Declarative Knowledge retained can be retrieved by the Learner

Figure 6.1: **Brain Based Learning**

Since a learning disability has a neurobiological foundation, application of recent findings regarding neurobiological learning can help to remediate many LD problems efficiently. Bigler

(1990) has demonstrated the positive application of neurobiological learning theory to the remediation of many non-verbal learning disabilities. Diaz (1992) is also working on cognitive teaching approaches that can positively affect the ability of individuals with learning disabilities to learn especially the use of "emotional teaching" experiences to facilitate strengthening of LTP (Diaz 1992, pp. 135-136).

In using brain based learning the cognitive and direct teaching methods are both applicable. The cognitive approach emphasizes the individual as an active learner in control of his learning situation, with the teacher inculcating in the student planning self-evaluation and self-monitoring skills. This method is usually incorporated in learning strategies approaches that are basically psychoneurological.

The direct teaching method emphasizes the active effort of the teacher to structure the student's environment. The direct teaching method includes (1) grouping immediate instructional needs; (2) sequencing academic skills to be remediated; (3) model successful academic practice; and (4) pacing academic skills that encourage many response opportunities.

Best Teaching Methods for LD Students

Various instructional approaches have proven to be beneficial for children with learning disabilities (Swanson, Carson & Sachse-Lee, 1996). In a meta-analysis of 78 intervention studies, it was reported that there was a mean effect size of 0.85, from a total of 324 effect sizes from this collection of studies on LD interventions ((Swanson, Carson & Sachse-Lee, 1996). This effect size provides significant support for the view that instructional interventions can positively affect the literacy of LD students.

A review of the LD intervention literature indicates that direct and cognitive instructional methods work well in the remediation of of learning disabilities. In a study of LD intervention literature between 1967 and 1993, Swanson, Carson, and Sachse-Lee (1996) reported a mean effect size score of 0.91 for direct instruction and 1.07 for cognitive teaching methods.

These findings indicating the success of direct and cognitive intervention strategies in the remediation of learning problems among children with learning disabilities were confirmed by Swanson and Hoskyn (1998). In a comprehensive meta-analysis of 180 intervention studies Swanson and Hoskyn (1998) report a 0.79 mean effect size for the experiemental intervention studies included in their study.

The meta-analysis of intervention literature by Swanson and Hoskyn (1998) make it clear that all academic learning disabilities are responsive to treatment. The mean effect size for this analysis of intervention instructional practices was 0.68 for direct instruction and 0.72 for cognitive teaching strategies (Swanson & Hoskyn, 1998). The high effect sizes for cognitive strategies instruction in the remediation of learning disabilities support the use of these strategies to enhance the academic achievement and performance of children with a learning disability.

Cognitive Instructional Methods

Because of the need to find a method to remediate the learning problems of students with a learning disability many educators early began to employ cognitive teaching strategies to improve the academic performance of students who are exceptional. Cognitive development is the human capacity to represent mentally objects and events existing in the real world (McShane, 1991, p.121). Wong and Wong (1988) have observed that:

"...the basic tenet in cognitive psychology, namely, the centrality of the student s' active participation in and responsibility for the learning" (p.26).

Cognitive teaching methods in special education are based on the paradigm of psychology--Skinner's notion of stimulus control, and the shaping and reinforcement of academic skills. The basic tenets of the cognitive teaching method are (1) the student must be an active participant in his learning, (2) students are responsible for their own learning, and (3) the teacher must inculcate in the students/ pupils planning, self-evaluation and self monitoring skills (Kavale, Forness, & Bender, 1988; Wong 1985a, 1985b, 1986; Wong & Wong 1988).

A computer model is used to describe the cognitive process. A computer has three components for : (1) input-output, (2) memory and (3) information processing. It also has a basic set of operations that execute specific programmed input-output functions.

The model for computer operations has been used to describe a learning disability. Using the computer model for learning disabilities, theoretically means that a learning disability is malfunction in the processing unit of the individual that adversely affects the manipulation of information, which causes faulty output of learned behavior.

The role of the cognitive system is to process, receive, retrieve and store information. The major components of the cognitive system are memory and attention (McShane, 1991, p.40). The foundation of cognitive development is the ability of humans to represent external events mentally (Bruer, 1994; McShane, 1991, p.121).

There are two principal mechanisms of learning: assimilation and accommodation. The process of assimilation is the process of interpreting new information based on established cognitive structures. Accommodation is the process that changes cognitive structures in response to the acquisition of new information (McShane, 1991, p.41). As a result of these mechanisms cognitive structures are modified over time.

Information is a stimulus from the environment that is perceived by an individual and processed by that individual's cognitive system. This means that environmental stimuli (information and knowledge) acts as input to the cognitive system.

Once the information is perceived it is encoded in the cognitive system. This encoded information exist in the cognitive system as the representation of the encoded input.

Pursuant to the cognitive theory for the functioning of the brain involves data structures. Data structures support the information representations in any given system (Crick, 1994).

Another term for representation is schema. Schemata are structures that store information about events, objects or situations that we have acquired (Bruer, 1994, p.26). These schemata also provide us with the structures to remember and interpret the stored information we have learned (Bruer, 1994, p.27). A representation or schema is an entity or state that represents an object and is interpretable .

This schemata is made up of mental representations that can be divided into three properties: format , content and organization in any processing system. Content is the information stored in any given data structure. Organization is simply the manner in which representations are formed. The format defines the (specific) elements that make up a representation or schema.

In general a representation or schema is the encoding of selective data concerning an external event or object. Recall is the output of a stored representation or memory.

Cognitive teaching methods seeks to help exceptional children learn based on their knowledge base or representations in the cerebral cortex. As a result, learning is the creation or modification of internal representations (Crick, 1994, p.66).

The cognitive teaching approach seeks to remediate the maladaptive and passive learning style of many children with learning disabilities. These children possess an external attribution system.

The cognitive approaches in special education include : (1) metacognition; (2) cognitive behavior modification; (3) cognitive training strategies; (4) advance organizer routines; (5) strategies intervention model and (6) verbal and visual cueing methods (Keller & Hallahan, 1987). Research indicate the successful transfer of learning strategy skills to mildly retarded students (Bruer, 1994, p.73).

Learning strategies are an effective method in teaching children with a learning disability because they involve the rehearsal of academic skills (Diaz, 1992; McShane 1991; Winters 1994, 1995).

Teaching students metacognition and learning strategies can make children with a learning disability more effective learners. They become more effective learners because they can increase the number of representations in the students knowledge base for future recall (Diaz, 1992; McShane, 1991, p.198). The students knowledge base or schema which determines the student's ability to learn.

Lev Vygotsky (1978) developed the idea that children can learn from their environment. He made it clear that children can learn from the people around them in their social environment.

Vygotsky (1978) believed that adults working with children can determine what that child learns. In this model of learning a child obtains optimum learning under the guidance of a nurturing mediator (a teacher). It was from his research that researchers developed the theoretical idea that social mediation may enhance the development of higher cognitive functioning (Vauras, Lehtinen, Kinnunen & Salonen, 1992).

Cognitive- metacognitive teaching models make the teacher the principle player in the transfer of metacognitive skills to the student during learning strategies training (Wong & Wong, 1988; Wong, 1992). Consequently, teaching metacognitive skills is a collaborative, social form of learning in which the teacher helps the student learn overt thinking and monitoring skills in a "public" forum , i.e., the classroom. This results in a positive instructional interaction between Vygotsky's model of social mediation and cognitive-metacognitive remediation (Baker & Brown, 1984; Palincsar & Brown, 1984; Stone & Wertach, 1984; Wood, Bruner,& Ross, 1976; Henderson, 1986). Thusly, metacognitive teaching interventions are able to remediate many learning deficits eventhough many leaning disabled children lack intrinsic attributional systems (Wong 1992).

In the metacognitive teaching approach the teacher provides a cognitive structure to learning (Palincsar and Brown, 1984; Brown & Campione, 1981, 1984). The teacher seeks to provide the student with the knowledge of his/her own self regulation and cognitive processes.

Bruer (1994, p.72) believes that metacognition makes a student a universal novice. Metacognition when taught to exceptional children provides them with the ability to predict one's ability to monitor their progress and increase their own problem solving skills.

In metacognitive instruction the teacher attempts to transfer metacognition skills to the student. Metacognition skills are covert and implicit when used by an instructor. The instructor's job is to make metacognitive skills overt and explicit through transfer to exceptional children .

The metacognitive teaching approach works well with one-to-one and small group instructional settings (Palincsar & Brown, 1984). Metacognitive teaching strategy calls on the teacher to provide cognitive structure to the student's learning. The teacher models the self evaluation procedures and review process to the student. S/he chooses the text for the student to read silently. The student is to assume more responsibility in their learning as they learn metacognition. Finally the student chooses his own text demonstrates the metacognitive process.

A major metacognitive strategy is the self monitoring of attention approach (SMAA). This is a cognitive behavior modification approach used to attack attentional problems of children with learning disabilities.

In the SMAA intervention the teacher discusses with the student his learning problem. The student listen to audiotapes which cue them to ask the question "Was I paying attention". The teacher models self-monitoring techniques. The student then monitors his own learning behavior (Wong & Wong, 1988).

The research indicates that SMAA is an effective with individuals and groups. It helps to increase a students attention. This teaching strategy worked well in remediating mathematics, reading, spelling and handwriting (Hallahan, Kneller & Lloyd, 1983).

A cognitive behavior modification approach is the self-questioning training (SQT) (Wong 1985a, 1985b, 1986). The SQT approach helps to improve reading comprehension. In this intervention the teacher's model's self-monitoring metacognition techniques during reading. The teacher teaches the student to ask the questions "What do I have to do?"; "Find the main idea/ideas in the paragraph an underline them"; "Check my work". these questions are generated by the student and the teacher (Wong & Wong, 1988).

The objective of SQT is to permit the student to use their intact strategies to comprehend reading. It will usually help the student to recall the main facts, manipulate active prior knowledge and monitor comprehension (Wong, 1985a, 1985b; Wong & Wong, 1988).

A principal method in cognitive teaching is the idea of constructivism. Constructivism, which is based on Jerome Bruners theory of discovery learning demand that the learner become actively involved in the construction of their own knowledge.

Cognitive constructivism is the internal construction of knowledge by the individual. It recognizes that knowledge is generative, since the learner will connect new knowledge to prior knowledge. As a result the individual constructs new understandings, and knowledge through his/her social interaction within a community of learners. This new knowledge is made into meaningful learning by the students completion of authentic tasks—tasks that relate the classroom experience(s) to the real world.

The constructivist model of teaching recognizes the need for students to become cognitive apprentices to learn effectively. This cognitive apprenticeship recognizes that students learn best when they are allowed to learn new knowledge in association with experienced learners, may they be teachers, peers, or parents, along as the learning relationship involves an Expert + Novice relationship. This promotes learning among students via modeling (learning through observation of a skilled learner); coaching (cognitive behavior guided by an expert); or scaffolding (teaching method where by the expert provides the novice learner support to accomplish his/her learning/tasks. Thusly, the teacher/expert models the learning for the novice, who must use metacognition and active participation in his/her own learning to make (or extend) his/her knowledge base.

Learning is a constructive process. This means that the learner makes an active effort to learn new knowledge. This phenomenon is related to intentional learning.

In a brain based special education learning environment we want to enhance the categorical memory functions of children with a learning disability so the representations or schema can be converted into procedural memories that can help the student with special needs to become a better reader or mathematician.

Brain based teaching calls on the student to produce his own knowledge individually and through cooperative learning communities or individually. Learning and knowledge created in this way is more meaningful for the student. Brain research makes it clear that children learn best when more than one sense modality is used when they learn. As a result, a multi-sensory learning environment offers the best environment for learning to take place in **communities of learners** (COLs). In these COLs, students construct their own knowledge.

Constructivist Theory

The constructivist approach to teaching favors brain based learning. It is congruent with brain based learning because it encourages children to think for themselves in social communities where they are reconstructing information, while previous knowledge is enriched through new learning experiences. The constructivist classroom satisfies this requirement. It meets this goal because it is a classroom where children are engaged in learning activities in which they play a direct role in their own learning. A role in which they work in learning communities to co-construct knowledge using their own hands, eyes, minds and mouths.

The constructivist classroom provides a stimulating learning environment that promotes learning and stimulation of many centers of the brain, which reflects the multiple centers of the brain, which carries out many learning experiences. This classroom, because the work is done by the students themselves, supports inquiry among children in social learning communities where they co-construct knowledge to create meaning out of their own learning.

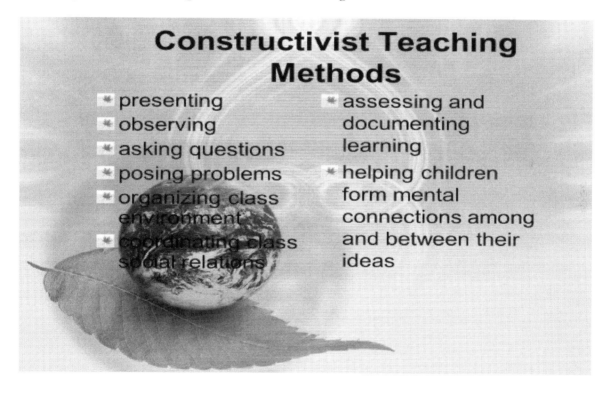

It is no secret that students in constructivists classrooms usually develop an hypothesis and pose questions that not only guide their learning, these theories and questions also relate learning to real life. This learning encourages students in the constructivist classroom to use all the senses to perform higher order thinking skills that determine agreed upon solutions to a problem; one that promotes neural branching. New learning experiences promote neural branching and greater retention and recall of the knowledge students' construct. The intellectual richness of the constructivist classroom supports brain based learning as children make their own meanings in a milieu of genuine discovery which ensures that what they learn is not quickly forgotten.

In brain based learning, the educator's objective is the development of a **community of learners**. Specifically, the teacher will employ some direct teaching methods, but the students will be required to use metacognition to construct their own knowledge.

> ### Students work in collaborative learning activities that encourage
> - Students will
> - Create self-knowledge
> - Develop autonomy in learning through interaction with their teacher and their peers.
> - Participate in learning activities that promote higher order thinking skills (HOTS)

Brain Based Learning

Student Role

Using the brain based learning, students will experience more engaged learning opportunities in which they will become more active learners and co-constructors of social science knowledge with their peers. As a result, the students will have many cooperative learning experiences in this course of study.

Using brain based learning students can take advantage of a variety of **cooperative learning settings**. Using brain based teaching methods; accommodations for special populations are made to help them become more efficient learners. The class participation of special students is increased when they work in groups because they are actively engaged in their own learning. Working in groups allow for accommodations based on size, time and participation. When students work in groups, the size of the workload and number of items that a learner is expected to learn is decreased. The "buddy system" allows the learner to share tasks. Using group presentation formats limits the pressures of time on many students with special needs, because students have a flexible time when assignments are due. Moreover, working in a group will allow special students time to collaborate with their regular education peers in a non-threatening environment. Increased collaboration between regular and special education students insures a more equitable learning situation, and gives greater support for all students in cooperative learning communities where students help each other to create knowledge.

The students are organized into COLs, which will include cooperative groups made up of pairs of students and three to four persons. Each student will assume different roles within the group: 1) Recorder, 2) Discussion leader, 3) Reporter, and 4) Taskmaster. The recorder will record the comments of the students. The discussion leader will keep the discussion flowing. The taskmaster will make sure that the group remains focused on the particular task chosen by the group, or assigned by the teacher. The reporter will report back to the class the results of the group conversations and research.

Two methods of grouping can work equally well. The first allows students to remain in the same group for the duration of the course of study, or if desired, the second group permits rotations on a lesson-by-lesson basis. Student roles in the COLs should change for each lesson. This will allow for active student involvement as making sure that you choose a different student to read each of the project-reports developed by the various groups.

Teacher Role

In cooperative learning, the teacher plays an important role in the instruction process. Although the teacher must play a passive role in the student's construction of knowledge, they still must play an active role as learning facilitator. In this role, the teacher must constantly move around the class to maintain the learning process in each group.

The teacher, as learning facilitator, will visit each group of students to make sure they are on task. Teachers help students remain on task by visiting each group and asking students questions about their project and how they are progressing in the completion of their task. In this way, teachers will monitor student metacognition toward completion of the cooperative project.

The projected timeframe for each group project will range between two and three forty-minute class periods. This will usually be necessary for students in each group to organize the material for presentation before the class. Additional time in the library, computer room and at home will be required to polish reports. The fruit of each group's research will be shared with the class.

Character Education

The brain based and cooperative learning instructional strategies are being used because COLs allow students to learn valuable character building skills. In the COL, each student is required to complete some part of the total project. This provides engaged learning opportunities for the learner, making it possible to self-create and co-construct authentic learning products. The ability of students to learn to work independently will help promote among our students, confidence and greater self-esteem.

While students are developing greater self-esteem in the COLs, they are also learning how to work cooperatively with others and to accept responsibility. Students are encouraged to demonstrate tolerance and flexibility in interpersonal and group situations. Student respect of himself/herself, other students and adults will be encouraged. Teachers work as teams to coordinate activities and thus model acceptable behaviors that students are encouraged to adopt. All of these factors make brain based learning a perfect way to promote character education through completion of the tasks in this module.

Another cognitive method used in special education is the cognitive behavior modification (CBM) approach (Polloway & Patton, 1989). The CBM approach is a self-cueing approach that inhibits inappropriate behaviors (Polloway & Patton, 1989, p.115).

The objective of CBM is to encourage behavior change through self-regulation or metacognition. The foundation of CBM is the idea that cognition controls behavior and that through alteration of one's thought processes may modify a students overt behavior.

The CBM model calls for the teacher to teach the student self-monitoring skills. It calls on the student learning categorization skills--the chunking of information to reduce memory load on the exceptional student. This teaching approach also encourages the student to develop an internal imager to comprehend representations/ schema already acquired and the ability to expertly learn and retain information by using rehearsal skills acquired during CBM.

Wong and Wong (1988) has outlined the constraints on the interpretation of metacognition on learning disabilities instruction. She argues that our inability to characterize a learning disability solely as a problem of metacognition is the major constraint on metacognitive teaching for some children. As a result metacognitive strategy training may improve performance but failure of an exceptional child to perform an academic task may best be resolved by an improved knowledge base or some other teaching approaches.

Although cognitive teaching methods are effective (Wong & Wong, 1988). Many cognitive gains fail to persist (Borkowski, Day, Saenz, Dietmeyer, Estrada & Groteluschen, 1992). There are a number of constraints on cognitive-metacognitive teaching. They include: (1) teaching an inappropriate metacognitive strategy to emediate a learning deficit; (2) lack of ability and effort on the part of the student to learn and perform a metacognitive skill; (3) a student may possess a basic decoding problems;and (4) non-cognitive variables including emotions, self-perception, belief systems and self-esteem can effect metacognitive abilities.

Borkowski, et al (1992, p.2) believe that these gains fail to be persistent for two reasons. One students do not enjoy and are not satisfied solely by the intrinsic rewards of successful academic performance. Secondly, metacognitive strategies are not joined with attention when tailoring interventions for children with learning disabilities. Given the failure of many exceptional children to retain the gains they learn in cognitive-metacognitive training; and the constraints on metacognitive instruction, make it clear that attributional training should accompany cognitive-metacognitive instruction in any brain based teaching program, to enhance the exceptional student's motivation to learn (Wong, 1992; Borkowski, et al, 1992). Possession of a positive motivational framework by exceptional students may make these students more conducive to the acquisition of metacognitively based data processing abilities.

To sum up this section, cognitive teaching methods can be very effective in the remediation of learning disabilities. These methods combine the social learning theories of Vygotsky and metacognition.

The research on the use of cognitive instructional methods in special education, makes it clear that exceptional children make tremendous gains using cognitive teaching methods (Wong, 1988; Keller & Hallahan, 1987). This research also illustrates that effective learning activities must be sensitive to the student's prior knowledge/ schemata and reflect eventual conditions of use of that knowledge.

The transfer of knowledge and skill to the exceptional student using the cognitive method make it necessary to teach the student knowledge and control of his own mental processes. This will help the exceptional student to become an active self-regulator of his learning. As a result, the special educator seeks to develop intelligent novices who use metacognition to improve and maintain what they have learned. Intelligent novices that use dialogue to make the learning strategies they have learned overt, explicit and concrete.

Moreover, even though there are constraints on cognitive-metacognitive teaching strategies, it is evident that they can be effective interventions for the exceptional child. But as educators we must remember that the cognitive teaching model is only one teaching method among many teaching approaches, that may help children with learning disabilities improve their academic performance.

The fact that MRIs indicated the possible location where cognitive functions were taking place relative to learning encouraged special educators to view several neuroscientific findings related to the brain applicable to special education ,including 1) that the brain learns best through repetition; 2) the emotionality of an experience influences retention; and 3) that the plasticity of the brain allows instructors the possibility to improve student memory ,attention and learning processes through mental exercises (Diaz,1992; Winters,1994, 1995).

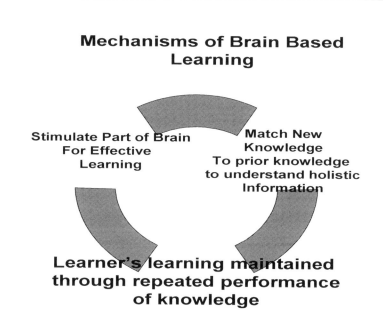

Figure 6.2: **Mechanism of Brain Based Learning**

Suggested Teaching Strategies

There is considerable research which suggest that neurobiological learning can improve language problems in children (Merzenich, et al, 1996; Pulvermuller 1995; Tallel, et al 1996). Michael Merzenich, et al (1996) and Paula Tallel, et al (1996) have used strategy trianing to remediate temporal processing problems in children with learning disabilities. The research of these scientist make it clear that cortical plasticity allows children with speech/phonemic perception problems to improve their language comprehension abilities (Merzenich et al 1996; Paula Tallel, et al 1996).

Research indicates that children with a reading disability suffer from dysfunction in the left hemispheric parietal-temporal cortical areas (Rourke 1985; Rourke, Bakker, Fisk & Strange 1983). The research of Tallel, et al (1996), Bigler (1992), and Merzenich, et al (1996) suggest that reading problems do not have to remain forever because neurological research indicates that new synapses can be formed through learning. As a result, many individuals that lose selected neuropsychological functions can recover (Bach-Y-Rita, 1990).

The research by neurobiological experts make it clear that special educators need to be made aware of the neurobiological origins of LD. The neurobiology of learning support the views of Myklebust (1964, 1968) regarding the CSN origins of learning disabilities. Most of the principles in teaching the learning disabled person is found in the neuropsychological approach of Helmer Myklebust.

Myklebust (1964,1968) developed a comprehensive theory of learning disabilities. Myklebust theorized that the brain was made up of semi-independent systems that either function in an independent or interdependent manner.

Myklebust's idea of interrelated systems modulating brain operations led him to develop his concept of interneurosensory learning, which can be defined as learning that "utilizes all these systems to functioning simultaneously" (Johnson & Myklebust, 1967, p.26). Some researchers have questioned the frequency of integrative learning (Myers & Hammil, 1991, p. 133). But today due to the dynamic research discussed above, we know that integrative learning is the primary model for neurobiological learning.

In integrative learning the teacher can obtain the best results from their instruction, it it is multisensory. In multisensory instruction the teacher encourages the learner to use more than one sensory perception while completing a learning task (Diaz, 1992; Winters, 1994).

Myklebust (1968; Johnson & Myklebust, 1967) made it clear that children should be process analyzed before their learning problem could be remediated. In this way the instructor could determine the LD child's deficits and develop the necessary learning plan to remediate his/her deficits.

Processing problems can be remediated due to the plasticity of the brain which allows corollary brain systems to form new neural pathways (Bach-Y-Rita, 1990). The presence of processing problems among children and adults with a LD or ADHD that hinder normal neuronal integration and/or growth of new synapses make the theories of Myklebust very relevant today.

Educators have been quick to believe that the notion of the brain plasticity, and the ability of external stimuli to produce representations-schemata that stimulate synaptic branching (as demonstrated by MRI blood flow activity during cognitive activity) supported the findings of Bandura=s concept of social learning and Vygotsky=s (1976) discovery of the role of ZPD in learning. Bandura and Vygotsky recognized that learning is a social phenomena,which involves the interaction between the learner and environmental factors such as other human beings teaching people with learning difficulties special strategies to remediate their learning problem.

Research and fMRI studies indicate that training students in phonics will help students become better readers. Restak (2003) observed that "It turns out that even highly skilled readers silently sound out words, especially unfamiliar words, while reading. Functional MRI activation of the lip and mouth areas in the primary motor cortex accompanies this silent reading" (p.184).

The student with a learning disability may not be able to hold the word in working memory long enough to link the beginning and ending of words or sentences. This suggest that active practice of word attack skills will help the poor reader to read more efficiently. Research suggest that after 80 hours of remedial reading instruction, providing students with phonemic awareness, and related skills, will make children and adults with a reading problem better readers (Restak,2003).

Bigler (1992, p. 502-503) reports that learning strategies can be effective in remediating learning disabilities. This results from the fact that one's long term memory is best established, when continually reinforced through practice. The continual reinforcement of a learned behavior will develop a stronger neural network, and smoother performance of the learned skill (strategy) taught by the special (and/or regular) educator.

Due to the neurobiological foundations of LD we can use the learning strategies and metacognitive approaches to provide the "repetitive treatment or practice" required by the cerebral cortex to reorder synaptic pathways. The reordering of the synaptic pathways will create new neural pathways that take over the function of underdeveloped, damaged or destroyed neural systems after learning has occurred (Bigler, 1992; Bach-Y-Rita, 1990; Winters ,1995).

To teach children with LD you must effectively control the learning environment. Brain research indicate numerous methods that may remediate some of the learning problems of children suffering from a learning difficulty.

The neuroscientific findings have led to the development of new ways of teaching special populations .Shaywitz (1996) used neuroscience to find a new method of teaching people with dyslexia to become better readers.

Shaywitz (1996) developed the phonological model for dyslexia based on the MRIs. The MRIs of dyslexics indicated to Shaywitz (1996) that many dyslexics fail to discriminate different sounds and as a result have a difficulty reading.
This finding using neuroscience methods helped him to recognize that by teaching some dyslexics phonemic awareness they could be more efficient readers.

 Numerous neurological and cognitive studies indicate that the emotionality of an experience can enhance the recall of a particular experience . The ability of emotional experiences to positively affect memory, which indicates neurobiological learning, suggest that neurobiological findings relating to emotional arousal and learning can, and should be applied to classroom instruction.

The research literature positively supports the view that the emotionality of an experience is a great predictor for the memorization of that experience. Using emotion laden slides or written passages , researchers have found significant support for the claim that emotional arousal causes the creation of vivid memories(Heuer & Reisberg 1990). These enhanced memories are probably associated with the modulation of the sympathetic nervous system and activation of the Adrenergic system (Cahill, Prins, Weber & McGaugh 1994).

Diaz (1992) is also working on cognitive teaching approaches that can positively affect the ability of individuals with ADHD and learning disabilities to learn more efficiently, especially the use of "emotional teaching" experiences to facilitate the strengthening of LTP (Diaz 1992). This will make learning more exciting.

Diaz (1992) theorized that since learning places considerable attention on one using their experiences to develop schemata-- which we interpret as learning-- experiences that have emotional content might facilitate greater recall and retention among learners who participate in emotion laden experiences. This research was confirmed by Winters (2003).

To test this hypothesis Diaz (1992) made up two list of words one containing neutral words and the other list made up of emotion laden words. These lists of words were presented to graduate students, and students from local elementary and high schools participating in the Chicago State University Special Education Instructional Laboratory. The results indicated in trial after trial that graduate and grade school students had greater recall of the emotion laden words than the neutral words (Diaz,1992). Other researchers report similar results for the use of emotion laden experiences in teaching (Caine, 1997; Diaz, 1992; Winters,1994,1995,2003; Wolfe & Brandt,1998).

Manipulatives and the combination of pictures with vocabulary items, also provide a good method to introduce a multisensory apprach to teaching. To make learning more exciting, teachers should use maniputatives and hands-on activities to increase the emotional arousal of children with a learning difficulty. Use emotionally arousal material, words and colors to increase the attention span of children with ADHD.

Nouns and verbs can be taught holistically when you use words and pictures. The words will stimulate auditory centers of the brain, while pictures will form new connections in the visual motor center.

An emotionally arousing picture of a word can be effective because emotional experiences can enhance memory (Cahill, Prins, Weber & McGaugh 1991). Knowledge that emotion can effectively make long term memory connections, helps us to find a specific mechanism to help the student with a learning disability learn more effectively.

In relation to reading it is clear that brain based teaching techniques will successfully make students with a reading disability better readers. "In short remedial programs can successfully reverse dyslexia", writes Dr. Restak (2003) reporting on research undertaken by doctors at the University of Texas Health Center at Houston, "as long as the program target the underlying problem—the dyslexic's diffuculty in grasping the correspondence between letters and phonemes. This approach, known as the alphabetic principle forms the structural underpinnings for teaching programs aimed at developing phonemic decoding skills" (p.181).

Figure 6.3: Reading Techniques based on Brain research.

A. Instructor should use
  1. more affective enactment
  2. affective/emotion laden words
  3. use affective reading material: Pets, Friends, & etc.
B. Affective Multisensory teaching

II. Synthetic Phonics and Word Attack Skills
  a. Use pictures
  b. Color coding

III. Whole Language Approach
  a. Develop affective stories about: Friends, family, pets, and etc.
    i. develop vocabulary for study
    ii. draw pictures
    iii. underline/ color code in text

Brain Based Learning and Math

To help students learn math we must take control of the reticular formation. The reticular formation is that part of the brain which is stimulated by visual and auditory stimulation. The reticular formation is a cluster of neurons in the brain stem. The reticular formation makes you aware of your environment. This is where you obtain your level of awareness.

The best way to "alert" the student is through motor activity which is the result of a physiological response. The

Concrete Action-Centered Multilevel Teaching method is the best way to make math easy for adolescents. Concrete action-centered multilevel teaching, put simply involves the use of manipulatives to encourage an explicit form of learning within students suffering from a math difficulty or math learning disability.

In arithematic the student must use both associative and working memory. Patricia S. Goldman-Rakic (1992) noted that "A simple activity involving working memory is the carry-over operation in mental arithematic, which requires temporarily storing a string of numbers and holding the sum of one addition in mind while calculating the next move" (p.111). A more complex example, is performing multiplication. In multiplication the student not only has to hold the multiplicand and the multiplier in the working memory, s\he also has to go into the long term memory to retrieve the product. This math knowledge is probably stored in the prefrontal cortex (Goldman-Rakic 1992).

Manipulatives help remediate adolescent math difficulties or math learning disabilities because they encourage use of the cognitive and direct teaching methods. The cognitive approach emphasizes the individual as an active learner in control of his learning situation, with the teacher and the manipulative inculcating in the student planning, self-evaluation and self-monitoring skills.

Manipulatives make learning less boring and brings about good feelings within the student. By attaching something interesting to the math experience, it helps the student remember better, especially if the math problem relates to actual experiences that adolescents might experience in their everyday lives. This is why you want to teach adolescents "real" Math problems that relate to their personal experiences.

We hypothesize three basic modalities in using manipulatives to correct adolescent math problems they are Demonstrate, Construct and Listen modes. They are:

(a) in the **Demonstrate** mode, the instructor illustrates to the learner the proper use of the manipulative, while the student **attends** to the instructor's directions.;

(b) in the **Construct** mode, the student physically manipu-lates an object or uses a pen or pencil to color in graphics, write numerals and etc.; and

(c) in the **Listen** mode, the instructor allows the student to both demonstrate and orally explain the procedures s/he performs during manipulation of the manipulatives. Use of these modalities by the adult learner, allows the learner to employ all the neurological processes while learning to perform math better.

We recommend that manipulatives can be used by teachers to enhance the math abilities of adults because they encourage repetitive performance of math skills that harden the LTPs. This strengthening of LTPs enables the learner to employ the use of both working and associative memory in overcoming a math disability. It also makes learning less boring while the student uses metacognition to remediate his math problems.

Learning math which involves the development of LTPs through repetitive strengthening of memories which constitute learned behaviors. This learning occurs when a student has the major prerequisites of learning good discrimination and memory skills.

Learning requires continuous practice. This means that the remedial student will only continue to show positive progress in over coming a reading problem through active practice of any reading strategy he has learned. This results from the fact that procedural knowledge is acquired after repeated practice (Crick, 1994). The neurobiological research makes it clear that if a neural circuit is not used you lose it.

In special education we want the categorical functioning of children with learning disabilities so their knowledge base can be converted into procedural memories that can help students with special needs become better learners. The research makes it clear that procedural memories relating to math ability, and reading: inferential reading, phonemic awareness, word attack skills and reading comprehension generally are enhanced when students have experienced learning strategies instruction (Crick, 1994).

Figure 6.4: Brain Based Math Teaching Techniques

a. Use songs to teach math facts

b. Color code: numerator/ denominator

c. Use manipulatives during instruction

In the regular classroom, the teacher spends a considerable amount of time encouraging students to perform multiple task. Over the years of my teaching in special education and regular classrooms, I have witness students being forced to learn too many concepts (especially) in math, only on a surface level, as they move from one concept to the next, without really ever practicing the math concept over an extended period of time.

To truly learn a concept students need time to master that concept through regular practice. This is especially true for students with a learning disability. Teaching one concept at a time is conducive to effective student learning. Restak (2003) explained that "In short, the brain is designed to work most efficiently when it works on a single task and for a sustained rather than intermittent and alternating periods of time" (p.58). This research supports the application of many of the brain based teaching methods when teaching students with a learning disability.

An understanding brain based learning provides the special educator with not only an understanding of the mechanism of learning (synapses formation and strengthening neural pathways); it also provides the teacher with the knowledge necessary to focus the instruction toward strengthening the weak neural circuit that may be causing a particular learning disability. In other words, using cognitive teaching methods the special educator directs his teaching toward weak synapses of the student with special needs, to strengthen these synapses, and make the learner mindful of his own ability to learn, and make (or reinforce) new connections in the brain that can help a student with a learning disability become a more efficient and effective learner.

Chapter 7: Common Core State Standards and Students with Disabilities

Common Core Standards were established to make learning to be open and accessible to different learners. Students with Disabilities (SwDs) are no exception they must be challenged to excel in the General Education and Separate classrooms where they receive their instruction so they can be prepared to be a success during their post school lives.

The Common Core State Standards are statements of what students should know and be able to do. The CCSS are Academic Achievement Standards developed by content areas and organized by grade with increasing complexity . As a result, CCSS Standards apply to all students, including students with disabilities.

In 1975 Public law 94-142, Individuals with Disabilities Act (IDEA) was created. This act made it clear that students with disabilities (SwD) would be provided a free and appropriate education. It required that school districts identify needs of students with special needs using nondiscriminatory assessment tools.

This public law attempted to increase parent involvement in Education decision making for SwD. And instead of requiring SwD to remain solely in the General Education classroom it called for the development of minimally restrictive learning environments which could include separate classrooms. To insure that SwD were properly educated the law demanded that teachers develop an individualized education program/plan (IEP) for SwD so their learning needs would be met.

The instruction SwD must be unique to the disability the child presents to the educator: his or her TEACHER. Even though the disability of each child may be different, IDEA supports the use of CCSS to educate SwD.

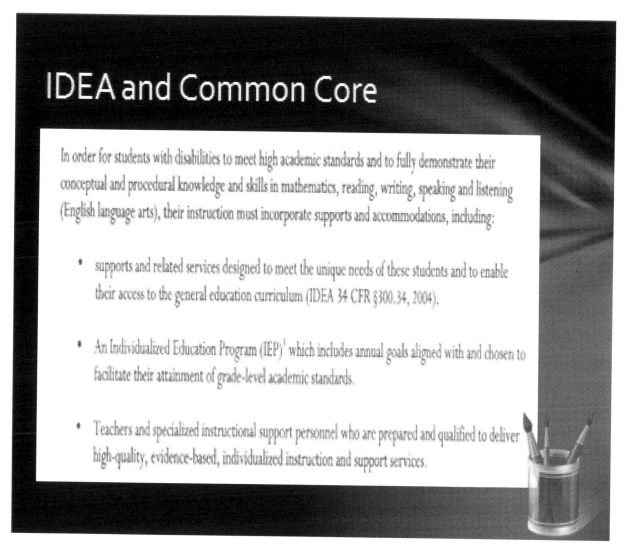

IDEA and Common Core

Promoting a culture of high expectations for all students is a fundamental goal of the Common Core State Standards. In order to participate with success in the general curriculum, students with disabilities, as appropriate, may be provided additional supports and services, such as:

- Instructional supports for learning— based on the principles of Universal Design for Learning (UDL)[2] —which foster student engagement by presenting information in multiple ways and allowing for diverse avenues of action and expression.

- Instructional accommodations (Thompson, Morse, Sharpe & Hall, 2005) —changes in materials or procedures— which do not change the standards but allow students to learn within the framework of the Common Core.

- Assistive technology devices and services to ensure access to the general education curriculum and the Common Core State Standards.

As a result of CCSS, supports and related services have to be developed to allow the SwD to access the general education curriculum by teachers who are qualified to provide their students with evidence-based, high-quality individualized instruction.

To participate in the Gen Ed curriculum there should be Instructional Accommodations made for slow learners and students with disabilities (SwDs). If needed SwDs should also have access to assistive technology devices and services.

Large gaps exist between the performance of SwD and their peers. Consequently SwDs should be provided learning strategies that can help them compensate for their individual disability and increase their knowledge base.

Use Formative Assessment to monitor student progress because: students—identify their strengths and weakness and target areas that need work.

Using CCSS, Educators can recognize where students are struggling and address problems immediately. Teaching is focused more effectively on the individual student. Positive effects may be particularly evident in lower performing students. As a result, learning in the wider (not subject-specific) sense can be enhanced.

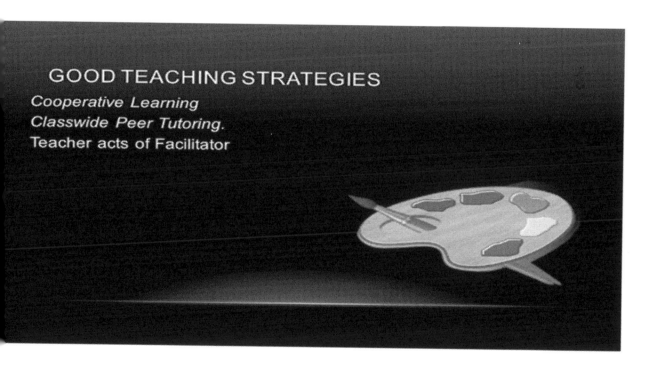

GOOD TEACHING STRATEGIES
Cooperative Learning
Classwide Peer Tutoring.
Teacher acts of Facilitator

There are a number of effective teaching methods used to educate SwDs, when using CCSS to develop reading and social studies units for instruction. Cognitive teaching methods are used to encourage SwDs become active learners, responsible for their own learning.

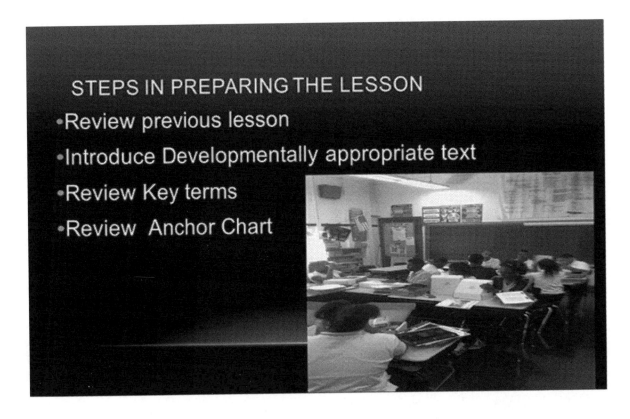

Using cognitive teaching methods SwDs take active control of the learning situation. The teacher has to plan the lesson so they can effectively transfer higher order thinking skills to their students.

Although direct instruction is necessary to teach SwD the numeracy skills and reading literacy, the teacher must inculcate in SwDs planning, self-evaluation and self-monitoring skills. Other effective teaching methods for SwD include:

- The Direct Teaching Method- which demands the active effort of teacher to structure student learning

- *Teacher groups immediate* instructional needs
- *Teacher sequences academic skills* to be remediated
- *Teacher models* successful academic practice
- *Teacher paces the transfer of academic skills*, to encourage students multiple opportunities to respond to learning tasks
- *Teacher provides immediate feedback*
- *Teacher provides frequent reinforcement* while monitoring student practice

Brain based teaching can also be used to effectively help SwD meet the rigorous CCSS. Using brain based teaching methods in e-pedagogy, accommodations for special population are made to help them become more efficient learners. To complete project based and problem based social science learning experiences, students will work mainly in communities of learning (COLs), with some assignments requiring individual work.

Common Core demands that students answer novel questions while they analyze documents, informational texts and artifacts.

Much of the work required of CCSS is done by the individual ; remember that class participation of special students is increased when they work in groups because they are actively engaged in their own learning.

There are limitations to using CCSS to teach SwD. These limitations are:

- The lines between academic skills and technical and life/employability skills are blurred
- They are not designed to cover every skill

- They were designed to provide basic skills instruction
- They are designed as foundation skills for post-secondary success

Even though using CCSS has its limitations working in groups provides SwDs accommodations based on size, time and participation. There are a number of reasons why SwDs working in groups is beneficial for their learning. When students work in groups, the size of the workload and number of items that a learner is expected to learn is decreased. The "buddy system" allows the learner to share tasks. Using group presentation formats limits the pressures of time on many students with special needs, because students have a flexible time when assignments are due.

Moreover, working in a group will allow SwD time to collaborate with their regular education peers in a non-threatening environment. Increased collaboration between regular and special education students insures a more equitable learning situation, and gives greater support for all students in cooperative learning communities where students help each other to create knowledge.

Final Word

In the earlier chapters we have reviewed research which indicates that children with a reading or a math disability suffer from right hemispheric visuoperceptual problems, or left hemispheric parietal-temporal cortical problems (Rourke, 1985; Bakker, 1990; Lyons, 1996b). This led Shaywitz (1996) to argue that dyslexia is the result of an "insufficiently developed phonological specialization" (p.101). Other research illustrates that the right parietal lobe influences self-awareness and the processing of visual spatial information. Children suffering from ADHD and learning disabilities share dysfunction in the right parietal lobe (Winters, 1994, 1995; Bigler, 1990,1992; Diaz, 1992). This may explain the large number of children diagnosed as learning disabled (Bain, 1991).

It appears that brain-based learning may be more than the latest educational fad. The fact that MRIs indicate the possible location where cognitive functions were taking place relative to learning encouraged special educators to view several neuroscientific findings related to the brain applicable to special education. Results suggested 1) that the brain learns best through repetition; 2) the emotionality of an experience influences retention; and 3) that the plasticity of the brain allows instructors the possibility to improve student memory, attention and learning processes through mental exercises (Diaz,1992; Winters,1994, 1995).

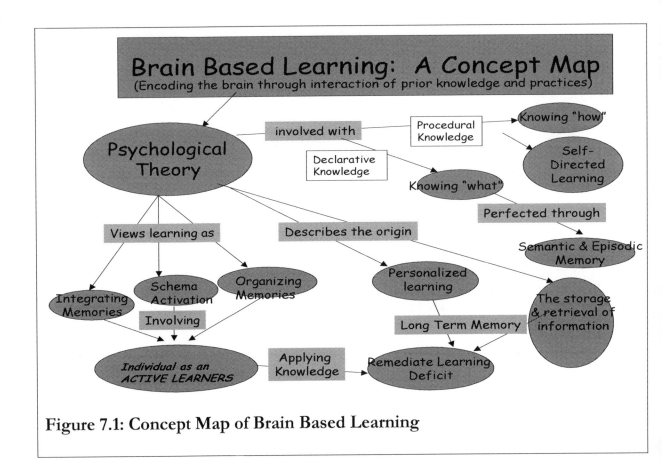

Figure 7.1: Concept Map of Brain Based Learning

Brain based teaching using cognitive teaching methods will bring about the Four Steps required for students with a learning disability to mindfully change their attitudes about learning, and ability to learn. There is promise in brain based learning, because we know the structure of the brain is constantly changing as we learn new knowledge (Restak, 2003; Schwartz & Begley, 2003; Winters, 2002). Restak (2003) wrote that "we now know that the brain never loses the power to transform itself on the basis of experience and this transformation can occur over very short intervals"(p.78).

The plasticity of the brain, the brains ability to transform itself as we experience the environment makes students with a learning disability capable of learning and perfecting what they learn through practice of the learned behavior or knowledge. This results from the principle of reinforcement, which simply means that as we practice a new behavior, repetition and use of the new knowledge will strengthen our ability to perform the tasks associated with the new knowledge we have learned (Restak, 2003).

If you want students with a learning disability to improve their abilities, these students have to practice, practice and more practice to reinforce what they have learned, so they can refine the mental representations or schema associated with the new knowledge base. The development of refined mental representations should allow the student to access and manipulate information more efficiently from the LTM (Restak, 2003). Better access to information in the LTM will naturally increase the performance of children with a learning disability because they will be taking advantage of the brain's plasticity to establish the necessary pathways to enhance their learning and academic performance.

In conclusion, as a result, of the neurobiological etiology of some children and adults exhibiting LD and ADHD disorders make it imperative that we understand the neurobiological origins of these learning deficits for accurate identification and treatment of these diverse disorders. The common denominator of ADHD and LD is the presence of a language disorder. The important role of the right hemisphere in extracting semantic information for graphemic analysis of the written word, suggest that problems in the right hemisphere can lead to language-based dysfunctions. The necessity of the right hemisphere in reading may explain the ADHD/LD comorbidity.

We have reviewed research which indicates that children with a reading or a math disability suffer from right hemispheric visuoperceptual problems, or left hemispheric parietal-temporal cortical problems (Rourke, 1985; Bakker, 1990; Lyons, 1996b). This led Shaywitz (1996) to argue that dyslexia is the result of an "insufficiently developed phonological specialization" (p.101). Other research illustrates that the right parietal lobe influences self-awareness and the processing of visual spatial information. Children suffering from ADHD and learning disabilities share dysfunction in the right parietal lobe (Winters, 1994, 1995; Bigler, 1990,1992; Diaz, 1992). This may explain the large number of children diagnosed as learning disabled (Bain, 1991).

The evidence of a neurobiological signature for many learning problems, and the neuroscientific evidence that the structure of the brain can be change through learning make it clear that teaching methods based on these findings may help learning disabled children and adults learn more efficiently. Now that we know more about brain structure and function, and the plasticity of the brain, this knowledge base can advise instructional interventions that can positively influence the ability of individuals with LD to learn more efficiently. For example, research indicates that the use of pictures to present words and nouns, and colors to write words create emotion (Diaz, 1992).

In general, the research indicates, especially MRI imaging, that teaching methods based on cognitive neuroscience can influence learning (Posner & Raichle, 1997; Shaywitz,1996) . For example, learning disabled students should be taught metacognition and provided more rehearsal time for their studies.

Whereas special educators have developed and or implemented teaching strategies based on the findings of cognitive neuroscience(Diaz, 1992; Winters, 1994,1995) , presently regular education brain based educators have not suggested any particular teaching methods (Wolfe & Brandt, 1998). This may be one of the reasons that brain based learning special education lacks support among most neuroscientists (Bruer,1997, 1998,1998b).

A cognitive perspective in the design and implementation of appropriate interventions in LD encourages the use of strategies training in the brain based or neurobiologically based instructional program of many students with identified as learning disabled. The use of cognitive teaching strategies in teaching the learning disabled reader, for example, can help them become self-regulating problem solvers who endeavor to play both a key and significant role in their own learning (McPhail & Palincsar, 1998). Research indicates that remediation of a redaing disability through cognitive teaching methods makes literacy more meaningful to the learner, as they use metacognition to monitor and overcome their reading processing problem (McPhail & Palincsar,1998; Swanson, Carson & Sachse-Lee, 1996; Swanson & Hoskyn, 1998).

The ability of new technology to provide instructors with insight into the processing problems experienced by people with a learning disability can inform future research. This makes it evident that future research should aim to develop, or identify and match existing learning strategies that can strengthen specific areas of the brain, to the specific disability of children diagnosed as ADHD and/or LD.

The evidence of a neurobiological signature for many learning problems, and the neuroscientific evidence that the structure of the brain can be changed through learning make it clear that teaching methods based on these findings can help learning disabled children and adults learn more efficiently. Now that we know more about brain structure and function, and the plasticity of the brain, this knowledge base can advise instructional interventions that can positively influence the ability of individuals with LD to learn more efficiently. For example, research indicates that the use of pictures to present words and nouns, and colors to write words create emotion (Diaz, 1992).

The ability of new imaging technology to provide instructors with insight into the processing problems experienced by people with a learning disability can inform future research. This makes it evident that future research should aim to develop, or identify and match existing learning strategies that can strengthen specific areas of the brain, to the specific disability of children diagnosed as ADHD and/or LD.

The research discussed above, indicates that cognitive teaching methods can be very effective in the remediation of learning disabilities. These methods combine the social learning theories of Vygotsky (1978)and metacognition. As a result, of the neurobiological etiology of some children and adults exhibiting LD and ADHD disorders make it imperative that we understand the neurobiological origins of these learning deficits for accurate identification and treatment of these diverse disorders. Once these deficits are identified we can then use cognitive teaching methods to remediate these learning problems.

Resources:

Assessing the Common Core and Students with Disabilities
http://ccsso.confex.com/ccsso/2010/webprogram/Presentation/Session1959/Assessing%20the%20Common%20Core%20and%20Students%20with%20Disabilities.pdf
Common Core Standards for all students in schools today requires thinking about their application for students with disabilities. How should accessibility issues be addressed - via accommodations, alternate assessments, or other means? What are the implementation challenges and opportunities, and the next steps to take in ensuring that students with disabilities benefit from the Common Core Standards?

Bring the Common Core to Life
http://vimeo.com/25206110
David Coleman, Founder and Chief Executive Officer, Student Achievement Partners, demonstrates two lesson plans - "Letter from a Birmingham Jail" and "Gettysburg Address" - that are aligned to the Common Core State Standards.

California Department of Education
http://www.cde.ca.gov/ci/cc/ccssfaqs2010.asp
Two possible timelines for implementation of California's Common Core State Standards (scroll down to FAQ #4 and click on *implementation of the CCSS.*"

CEC Today (Council for Exceptional Children)
http://www.cec.sped.org/AM/Template.cfm?Section=CEC_Today1&TEMPLATE=/CM/ContentDisplay.cfm&CONTENTID=15269
Common Core Standards: What Special Educators Need to Know

Common Core's Implications for Special Ed Students
http://www.districtadministration.com/viewarticle.aspx?articleid=2693
Common Core's Implications for Special Ed Students

Common Core State Standards
http://www.corestandards.org/the-standards
Application to Students with Disabilities This document – formulated with substantial input by disability organizations in Washington, seeks to clearly establish that IDEA-eligible students are to be given the same opportunity to learn these standards as all other students. The exception is that they need all of the specialized services and supports required by IDEA.

REFERENCES

Atikinson, R.C. & Shiffrin, R.M. (1971). The control of short term memory. Scientific American, 225 (2), 82-90.

Atkinson, R.C. & Shiffrin, R. M. (1968). Human memory: A proposed system and its control processes. In K. W. Spence & J. T. Spence (Eds.) Advances in the psychology of learning and motivation, vol. 2. New York: Academic Press.

Bach-T-Rita, P. (1990). Brain plasticity as a basis for recovery of functions in humans. Neuropsychologia, 28, 547-554.

Bain, L.J. (1991). A parent's guide to attention deficit disorder. New York: Dell.

Baker, L. & Brown, A.L. (1984). Metacognitive skills and reading. In P.J. Pearson, R. Barr, M.L. Kamil, & P. Mosenthal (Eds.), Handbook of Reading Research (pp.353-394). New York: Longman.

Bakker, D.J. (1990). Neuropsychological treatment of dyslexia. New York: Oxford University Press.

Bakker, D.J. & Licht, R. (1986). Learning to read: Changing horses mid-stream. In G.T. Pavlidis & D.F. Fisher (Eds.) Dyslexia: Neuropsychology and treatment (pp. 87-95). London: Wiley.

Barley, R.A. (1990). Attention-deficit hyperactivity disorder: A handbook for diagnosis and treatment. New York: Guilford Press.

Berninger, V.W. (1994). Reading and Writing Acquisition. Boulder, Colorado: Westview Press.

Bigler, E.D. (1990). Remediating Nonverbal problems associated with learning disabilities. In P.T. Myers & D. D. Hammil, Learning Disabilities, (ed.)(Austin, TX:Pro-Ed), 321-349.

Bigler,E.D. (1992). The neurobiology and neuropsychology of adult learning disorders. Journal of Learning Disabilities, 25 , 488-506.

Bonnet, K.A. (1989). Learning disabilities: A neurobiological perspective in Humans. Remedial and Special Education, 10, 8-19.

Brandt,R. (1997). On using knowledge about our brain: A conversation with Bob Sylvester. Educational Leadership, 54(6), 33-37

Borkowski, J.G., Day, J.D., Saenz, D., Dietmeyer, D., Estrada, T.M. & Groteluschen,A. (1992). Expanding the boundaries of cognitive interventions. In. B.Y.L. Wong (Ed.), Contemporary Intervention Reseach in Learning Disabilities (pp.1-21). New York: Springer-Verlag.

Brown, A.L., Campione, J.C., and Day, J.D. 1981. Learning to learn: On training students to learn from texts. Educational Researcher, 10, 14-21.

Brown, A.L., Campione, J.C., & Bradley, L.R. (1979). Training self-checking routines for estimating test readiness: Generalization from list learning to prose recall. Child Development, 50, 501-512.

Bruer, T.J. (1998). Brain science, brain fiction.Educational Leadership,56 (3), 14-18.

Bruer, T.J. (1998b).Let's put brain science on the back bruner. NASSP Bulletin, 82(598), 21-28.

Bruer,T.J.(1997). Education and the brain:A bridge too far. Educational Researcher, 26(8), 4-16.

Bruer, T. J. (1993). Schools for Thought. Cambridge, Mass. : MIT Press.

Byrnes, J.P. (2001). *Cognitive development and learning: In instructional contexts*. Boston: Allyn and Bacon.

Cahill,L, Prins, B, Weber, M. & McGaugh,J. (1994). B-Adrenergic activation and memory for emotional events. *Nature, 371*, 702-704.

Cawley,J.F.,Kahn,H.,& Tedesco,A.(1989). "Vocational Education and Students with Learning Disabilities". *Journal of Learning Disabilities*, 22, no.11, 630-640.

Caine, R.N. & Caine,G. (1997). *Education on the edge of possibilit*.Alexandria, Va.: ASCD.

Cardellichio,T & Field. (1997). Seven startegies that encourage neural branching. *Educational Leadership*, 54(6), 33-37.

Cohn,R. (1961). "Dyscalculia". *Arch. Neurol.*, 4:301-307.

Cohn,R.(1968). "Developmental dyscalculia". *Ped. Clin. N.Amer.*, 15:651-668.

Cramer, S.C. & Ellis, W. (1996). *Learning Disabilities: Lifelong issues*. London, Paul H. Brookes Pub. Co.

Crick, Francis. (1994). *The astonishing hypothesis: The scientific search for the soul*. New York: Touchstone Books.

Diaz,A.M. (1992). *The thinking brain: The neurobiology of learning and learning problems for teachers and parents.* Chicago: Chicago State University, Special Education Department.

Fletcher,J.M., Shaywitz,S.E., Shankweiter, D.P., Katz, L., Lieberman, I.Y., Stuebing,K.K., Francis, D.J., Fowler,A.E. & Shaywitz, B.A. (1994). Cognitive profiles of reading disability: Comparisons of discrepancy and low achievement definitions. *Journal of Educational Psychology, 86* (1), 6-23.

Filipek, P., & Kennedy, D. (1991). Magnetic resonance imaging:Its role in developmental disorders. In D.D. Duane & D.B. Gray (Eds.), The reading brain: The biological basis of dyslexia (pp. 133-160). Parkton,MD: York Press.

Fisk, J.L. & Rourke, B.P. (1979). Identification of sub-types of learning-disabled children at three age levels: A   neuropsychological, multivariate approach. Journal of Clinical Neuropsychology, 1, 289-310.

Fletcher, J.M. & Shaywitz, B.A. (1996). Attention deficit /Hyperactivity Disorder. In S.C. Cramer & W. Ellis (Eds.) , Learning disabilities: Lifelong issues (pp. 265-276). Baltimore: Paul H. Brookes Publishing.

Goldman-Rakic,P.S. (1992). Working Memory and the Mind, Scientific American , 268 (9), 111-115.

Goodyear, P. & Hynd, G.W. (1992). Attention-deficit disorder with (ADD/H) hyperactivity and without (ADD/WO). Journal of Clinical Child Psychology, 21, 273-305.

Gross-Glenn,K., Duara, R., Yoshii, F., Baker, W., Chen, Y., Apicella, A., Boothe, & Lubs, H. (1986). PET-scan studies during reading in dyslexic and non-dyslexic adults. Society of Neuroscience, Abstracts, 12, 1364.

Grady, M.P. (1984). Teaching and Brain Research. New York:Longman.

Hallahan, D.P., Hall,R.J., Ianna, S.O., Kneedler, R.D., Lloyd, J.W., Loper, A.B., and Reeve,R.E. (1983). "Summary of research findings at the University of Virginia learning disabilities Research Institute. Exceptional Children, 4 (1), 95-114.

Hallahan, D.P. and Kauffman, J.M. (1977). Labels, categories, behaviors:ED, LD, and EMR reconsidered. Journal of Special education, 11, 139-49.

Hallahan, D.P., Kneedler, R.D., and Lloyd, J.W.(1983). Cognitive behavior modification techniques for learning disabled children: self-instruction and self-monitoring. In Current Topics in Learning Disabilities, (Eds.) J.D. McKinney and L. Feagans. Vol.1. Norwood,N.J.: Ablex.

Hansen,L.(2002). Brain development, structing of learning and science education:where are we now? A review of some recent research. International Journal of Science Education, 24(4), 343-356.

Hebb, D.O. (1964). Organization of behavior. New York: John

Henderson, R.W. (1986). Self-regulated learning: Implications for the design of instructional media. Contemporary Educational Psyhology, 11, 405-427.

Hodgkinson,H.L.(1989). The Same Client:the Demographics of Education and Service Delivery Systems.Washington,D.C.: Institute for Educational Leadership, Center for Demographic Leadership.

Hooper, S.R. , Hynd, G.W. & Tramontana, M.G. (1988). Visual- spatial dyslexia: A neuropsychological case report, Neuropsychology , 2, 135-143.

Hulme, C. (1992). Working memory and severe learning difficulties-essays in cognitive psychology. East Sussex, United Kingdom: Erlbaum.

Johnson,D.S. & Myklebust, H.R. (1967). Learning disabilities: Educational principles and practices. New York: Grune & Stratton.

Jones,R. (November,1995).Smart brains.The American School Board Journal, 22-26.

Kandel, E.R. & Hawkins, R.D. (1992). "The biological basis oflearning and individuality", Scientific American, no.9,pp.79-85.

Kavale, K.A., Forness, S.R. & Bender, M. (1988). Handbook of Learning Disabilities: Methods and Interventions. Boston: Little Brown and Company.

Keller, C.E. (1987). Learning Disabilities: Issues and Instructional Interventions. Washington, D.C.: National Education Association.

Kirk, S.A., & Gallagher, J.J. (1989). Educating Exceptional Children. Boston: Hoghton Miffin Company.

Kolb, B. & Whishaw, I.Q. (1990). Fundamentals of human neuro-psychology. New York: W.H. Freeman & Company.

Leiberman, I.Y., Shankweiler, D., Fischer, F.W. & Carter, B. (1974). Explicit syllable and phoneme segmentation in the young child. Journal of Experimental Child Psychology, 18, 201-212.

Lerner, J.W. (1988). Learning Disabilities. Boston: Houghton Miffin Company.

Lubs, H., Duara, R., Levin, B., Jallad, B., Lubs, M.L., Rabin, M., Kushch, A., & Gross-Glenn, K. (1991). Dyslexia subtypes: genetic behavior, and brain imaging. In D.D. Duane & D.B. Gray, The reading brain: The biological basis of dyslexia (pp.89-118). Parkton, MD: York Press.

Luria, A. R. (1973). The working brain: An introduction to neuropsychology. New York: basic Books.

Lyon, G.R. (Ed.). (1994). Frames of reference for the assessment of learning disabilities: New views on measurement issues. Baltimore: Paul H. Brookes Publishing Co.

Lyon, G.R. (1996). Foundations of neuroanatomy and neuropsychology. In G. R. Lyon & J.M. Rumsey (Eds.), Neuro-imaging: A window to the neurological foundations of learning and behavior in children (pp.3-23). Baltimore: Paul H. Brookes Publishing Co.

Lyon, G.R. (1996b). The state of research. In S. C. Cramer & W. Ellis (Eds.), Learning disabilities: Lifelong issues (pp.3-64). Baltimore: Paul H. Brookes Publishing Co.

Lyon, G.R. & Moats, L.C. (1993). An examination of research in learning disabilities: Past practices and future directions. In G.R. Lyon, D. B. Gray, J.F. Kavanaugh & N.A. Krasnegor (Eds.), Better understanding learning disabilities: New views from research and their implications for education and public policies (pp. 1-14). Baltimore: Paul H. Brookes Publishing Co.

Lyon, G.R. & Rumsey, J. (Eds.). (1996). Neuroimaging: A window to the neurological foundations of learning and behavior. Baltimore: Paul H. Brookes Publishing Co.

Lyon, G.R., Stewart, N., & Freedman,D. (1982). Neuropsychological characteristics of empirically derived subgroups of learning disabled readers. Journal of Clinical Neuropsychology, 4, 343-365.

Lynch, G. & Baudry M.(1984). "The Biochemistry of Memory:A new and specific hypothesis", Science, 224 , pp.1057-1063.

79-85.

Levy, J. (1977). The mammalian brain and the adaptive advantage of cerebral asymmetry. Annals New York Academy Sciences, 299, 264-272.

Licht,R. (1988). Event-related potential asymmetries and word reading in children: A developmental study. Unpublished doctoral dissertation. Free University, Amsterdam.

Lynch, G. & Baudry M.(1984). The Biochemistry of Memory:A new and specific hypothesis, Science, 224 , 1057-1063.

McKean,K.(1983). Memory, Discover ,no.11, pp.19-27.

McGilly,K. (Ed.). (1996). Classroom lessons: Integrating cognitive theory and classroom practice. Cambridge,Mass.: The MIT Press.

McPhail, J.C. & Palincsar, A.S. (1998). The research of understanding of learning disabilities: A response to Kavale and Forness, Learning Disabilities Quarterly, 21 (4), 297-305.

McShane, J. (1991). Cognitive Development. Cambridge, Mass: Basil Blackwell, Inc.

Moats, L.C. & Lyon, G.R. (1993). Learning disabilities in the United States: Advocacy, science, and the future of the field. Journal of Learning Disabilities, 26, 282-294.

Myers, P.I., & Hammill, D.D. (1990). (Eds.) Learning Disabilities. Austin, TX: Pro-Ed.

Myklebust, H.R. (1964). Learning disorders: Psychoneurological disturbances in childhood. Rehabilitation Literature, 25, 354-359.

Myklebust, H.R. (1968). Learning disabilities: Definition and overview. In H.R. Myklebust (Ed.), Progress in learning disabilities (Vol. 1, p. 1-15). New York: Grune & Stratton.

Myklebust, H. R. (1975). Nonverbal learning disabilities: Assessment and intervention. In H. R. Myklebust (Ed.), Progress in learning disabilities Vol. 3, (85-121). New York Guilford.

Novick, B.Z. & Arnold, M.M. (1988). Fundamentals of clinical child neuropsychology. New York: Grune & Stratton.

Palincsar, A.S. & Brown, A.L. (1984). Reciprocal teaching and comprehension-fostering and comprehension-monitoring activities. Cognition and instruction, 1, 117-175.

Polloway, E.A. & Patton, J.R. (1989). Strategies for teaching learners with special needs. New York: Merrill.

Pontius, A.A. (1973). Dysfunction patterns analogous to frontal lobe system and caudate nucleus syndromes in some groups of minimal brain dysfunction. Journal of American Medical Women's Association, 28 ,285-292.

Pool, C.R. (1998). Maximizing learning.Educational Leadership, 54(5), 11-15.

Posner, M.I & Raichle, M.E. (1997). Images of the Mind. New York: W.H. Freeman and Company.

Prigge,D.J. (2002). 20 ways to promote brain-based teaching and learning. Intervention In School and Clinic, 37 (4), 237-41.

Restak,R.(2003). The new brain. New York, N.Y.: Rodale.

Rothstein,A. & Crosby,M. (1989). Learning Disorders:An Integration of Neuropsychological and Psychoanalytic Consideration. Madison: International Universities Press, Inc.

Rourke, B.P. (1978). reading, spelling, arithmetic disabilities: A neuropsychological perspective. In H.R. Myklebust (Ed.), Progress in learning disabilities (Vol. 4, pp.97-120). New York: Grune & Stratton.

Rourke, B.P. (1985).(Ed.) Neuropsychology of Learning Disabilities. New York: The Guilford Press.

Rourke, B. P. & Strang,J.D. (1984). Subtypes of reading and arithematical disabilities: A neuropsychological analysis. In M. Rutter (Ed.),Developmental neuropsychiatry , (473-488) New York: Guilford.

Schwartz, J.M. and Begley, S. (2003).The mind and the brain. New York, N.Y.: HarperCollins Publishers, Inc.

Shaywitz, S.E. (1996). Dyslexia. Scientific American, 275 (5), 98-105.

Shaywitz, B.A., Shaywitz, S.E., Byrne, T., Cohen, D.J. & Rothman, S. (1983). Attention deficit disorder. Quantitative analysis of CT. Neurology, 33, 1500-1503.

Shaywitz, S.E. & Shaywitz, B.A. (1996). Unlocking learning disabilities: The neurological basis. In S. C. Cramer & W. Ellis (Eds.), Learning disabilities: Lifelong issues (pp. 255-260). Baltimore: Paul H. Brookes Publishing Co.

Shafrir, U. & Siegel, L.S. (1994). Subtypes of learning disabilities in adolescents and adults. Journal of Learning Disabilities, 27 (2), 123-134.

Shelton, T.L. & Barkley, R.A. (1994). Critical issues in the assessment of attention deficit disorders in children. Topics in Language disorders, 14, 26-41.

Siegel, L.S. & Heaven, P.K. (1986). Categorization of learning disabilities. In S.J. Ceci (Ed.), Handbook of Cognitive social and neuropsychological aspects of learning disabilities Vol. 1 (pp. 95-121). Hillsdale, N.J.: Erlbaum.

Silver, L.B. (1990). Attention deficit-hyperactivity disorder: Is it a learning disability or a related disorder? Journal of Learning Disabilities, 23, 394-397.

Spreen, O. & Haaf, R.G. (1986). Empirically derived learning disability subtypes: A replication attempt and longitudinal pattern over 15 years. Journal of Learning Disability, 19, 170-180.

Stone, A.C. & Wertach, J.V. (1984). A social interactional analysis of learning disabilities remediation. Journal of Learning Disabilities, 17, 194-199.

Strang, J.D. & Rourke, B.P. (Eds.) (1985). "Arithmetic Disability subtypes: The Neuropsychological Significance of Specific Arithmetical Impairment in childhood". In J.D. Rourke (Ed.) Neuropsychology of Learning Disabilities, (New York: The Guilford Press), 167-183.

Swanson, H.l. Carson,C. & Sachse-Lee,C.M. (1996). A selective synthesis of interventio n research for students with learning disabilities, School Psychology Review, 25, 370-391.

Swanson, H.L. & Hoskyn,M. 1998. Experimental intervention research on students with learning disabilities: A meta-analysis of treatment outcomes. Review of educational Research, 68 (3), 277-321.

Shaywitz,B.A. (1997). The Yale center for the study of learning and attention: Longitudinal and neurobiological studies, Learning Disabilities: A multidisciplinary Journal, 8 (1), 21-29.

Terry,W.S. (2003). Learning and memory. New York: Pearson Education, Inc.

U.S. Office of Education. (1977). Assitance to states for education of handicapped children:Procedures for evaluating specific learning disabilities. Federal Register, 42, 65082-65085.

USDE. (1995). To assure the free appropriate public education of education of all children with disabilities. Washington, D.C: U.S. Department of education.

Van Strien, J.W., Stolk, B.D. & Zuiker, S. (1995). Hemisphere-specific treatment of dyslexia subtypes: Better reading with anxiety-laden words? Journal of Learning Disabilities, 28(1), 30-34.

Vauras, M. (1991). Text learning strategies in school-aged students. Annales Academia Scientiarum Fennica, Dissertationes Humanarum Litterarum, 59. Helsinki: Academia Scientarum Fennica.

Viadero,D. (18 September,1996). Brain trust. Education Week, 31-33.

Voeller, K.K.S. (1991). Toward a nerobiologic nosology of attention deficit disorder. Journal of Clinical Neurology, 6S , S2-S8.

Vygotsky,L.S. (1978). Mind in society. Cambridge, M.A.: Harvard University Press.

Winters, C.A. (May 1994). The applications of neurobiological research in special education instruction. Thresholds in Education , 36-42.

_____. (1995). Neurobiological learning and adultliteracy. Columbus, Ohio: ERIC Clearinghouse on Adult, Career and

Vocational Education. (ERIC Documentation Reproduction Service No. ED 385 740).

_____. (1999). <u>The potential impact of the neurobiological knowledge base on the education of the learning disabled.</u> 1999 Annual meeting of the American Educational Research Association. Montreal, Canada.

_____.2000."Making math easy for the learning disabled adolescents: Neurobiology and the use of math manipulatives. <u>Review Journal of Philosophy and Social Science,</u> 25 (1&2), 58-68.

_____.2000. Neurological Basis Cognition, Emotion and Classroom Instruction. <u>Research Journal of Philosophy and Social Sciences,</u> 25 (1&2), 39-44.

_____.2002. Brain based learning and special education. In Thomas E. Deering (Ed.), <u>Teacher Education</u> (pp.128-167), Anu Books, Shivaji Road, Meerut India (ISBN: 81-85126-91-7).

_____.2003. Popular culture, critical pedagogy and the African American Print Media". In James J Van Patten (Ed.) The future of Education Issues & Trends (pp.164-184), Anu Books, Shivaji Road, Meerut India (ISBN: 81-85126-102-7)

_____.(2003).Emotion, neurobiological learning and classroom instruction, Research Journal of Philosophy and Social Science,No.1-2, pp.23-34.

_____.(2005). Teaching matters: Phonological Brain based teaching methods and reading improvement. Research Journal Philosophy & Social Science, 31 (1-2), 33-46.

_____.(2005). Informed Insight: Parental Attitudes Toward Technology. Tech Learning, February. Retrieved 2/1/05 at: http://www.techlearning.com/showArticle.jhtml?articleID=57702734

_____.(2005). Dewey and the organization of learning on the World Wide Web. In Midwest Philosophy of Education Society:

Proceedings of Midwest Philosophy of Education Society Annual Conferences 2001-2003, (ED.) O. Jagusah, D. Smith, A. Makedon (pp. 565-575). Author House, Bloomington, IN. 47403.

_____.(2005). Predator or Victim: The role of correctional education, offender habitation and democracy. In Midwest Philosophy of Education Society: Proceedings of Midwest Philosophy of Education Society Annual Conferences 2001-2003, (ED.) O. Jagusah, D. Smith, A. Makedon (pp. 576-593). Author House, Bloomington, IN. 47403.

_____.(2005). Closing the Gap. Letter to Editor, GDW-G EDTECH, Winter 2004. Retrieved 3/3/05. Http://edtech.texterity.com/article/200411/6/

_____.(2006).The Dilemma of School Anti-Harassment Policies and the First Amendment. Journal on Educational Controversy. Retrieved 2/23/2006. http://www.wce.wwu.edu?Resources?CEP/eJournal/V001n001/a003.shtml

_____.(2006). E-Pedagogy and the Student Social Science Research Community. Review Journal of Philosophy and Social Science, 31, 1&2, 75-104.

_____Brain based learning and special education. In Thomas E. Deering (Ed.), Teacher Education (pp.128-167), Anu Books, Shivaji Road, Meerut India (ISBN: 81-85126-91-7)

_____Emotional Intelligence and Teaching. Proceedings of the 2004-2005 Midwest Philosophy of Education Society (pp.341-356) ,2007.

_____(2007).Ignite Student Learning:Insights from a Neurologist and Classroom Teacher, in the TCRecord , 16 February 2007.

_____(2007).Planning for Disaster Education Policy in the Wake of Hurricane Katrina, Multicultural Education,15(2) (2007): 39-42.

Wolfe, P. & Brandt, R. (1998). What do we know from brain research. Educational Leadership, 56(3), 8-13.

Wong, B.Y.L. (1985a). Metacognition and Learning disabilities. In D.L. Forrest-Pressley, G.E. MacKinnon, and T. G. Waller (Eds.), Metacognition, cognition and human performance (Vol.2, pp.137-180). Orlando, FL.: Academic Press.

Wong, B.Y.L. (1985b). Self questioning instructional research: A review. Review of Educational Research, 55, 227-268.

Wong, B.Y.L. (1986). Metacognition and special education: A review of a view. Journal of Special Education, 20, 9-20.

Wong, B.Y.L. (Ed.). (1992). Contemporary intervention research in learning disabilities: An international perspective. New York: Springer-Verlag.

Wong, B.Y.L., & Wong, R. (1988). Cognitive, intervention for learning disabilities. In Kavale (Ed.), Learning disabilities: State of the art and practice (pp.141-160). Boston: College-Hill Publication.

Wood, F.B. (1990). Functional neuroimaging in neurobehavioral research. In A.A. Boulton, G.B. Baker, & M. Hiscock (Eds.), Neuromethods: Vol.17. Neuropsychology (pp.65-89). Clifton, N.J.: Humana Press.

Wood, F.B., Felton, R., Flowers,L., & Naylor, C. (1991). Neurobehavioral definition of dyslexia. In D.D. Duane & D. B. Gray (Eds.), The reading brains: The biological basis of dyslexia (pp. 1-26). Parkton, MD: York Press.

Ysseldyke,J.E., Algozzine,B. & Thurlow,M.L. (1992) Critical Issues in Special Education. Boston Houghton Miffin Com.

ABOUT THE AUTHOR

Clyde Winters Ph.D, is Director of the Uthman dan Fodio Institute. He has taught Education and Linguistics courses at Saint Xavier University.

Dr. Winters is the author of numerous articles and books on education, ancient history anthropology and archaeogenetics.. His work has appeared in the Journal of Black Studies, Afrique Historique, Journal of African Civilization, Adolescence, International Review of Education, Yearbook of Correctional Education, The Journal of Correctional Education, Thresholds in Education, Ancient Origins and TCRecord to name a few. Presently, he is working on methods to make brain based learning strategies an effective tool in improving the academic achievement of regular and special needs students.

End Note

1. The teaching methods of Myklebust and Johnson do have several deficits. These deficits include the fact that the test are given in an individualized setting and teaching is also individualized. This is a good approach but in most classrooms even with the assistance of an aide, it is very difficult to spend considerable amounts of teaching time with one child. The second deficit in the Myklebust and Johnson theory is that Myklebust makes the assumption that

brain damage is evidenced in children who are psychologically tested and present LD problems. This view often is invalid , an LD problem may not be evidence of neurological damage within children that have an LD problem, even though these children may have centers in the brain that are not being used or lack maturation. This lack of maturation or lack of use may encourage the presence of a learning problem in some children, not. neurological damage

Made in the USA
Middletown, DE
25 July 2019